SITE TO INSAT

Challenges of Production and Research for
Women and Children

About the Editors

Binod C. Agrawal (Ph. D. Wisconsin) is responsible for conducting social impact studies of various programmes of ISRO. He taught at Iowa State University and at the Indian Agricultural Research Institute, Delhi. He has several publications- books and papers in international journals - to his credit. Dr. Agrawal organized the X International Congress of Anthropological and Ethnological Science (1978) and is responsible for organizing the 15th International Association of Mass Communication Research General Assembly and Conference (1986).

Arbind Sinha (Ph. D. Vik) is one of the few scholars who continues to work in the field of communication since the days of Satellite Instructional Television Experiment. He contributed papers in several national and international journals. His publications include Mass Media and Rural Development (1985) and SITE to INSAT (1986). He organized sessions in X International Congress of Anthropological and Ethological Science (India, 1978) and the XI Congress (Canada, 1983). Dr. Sinha has also established himself in the field of disaster communication.

SITE TO INSAT

Challenges of Production and Research for Women and Children

Edited by
Binod C. Agrawal
Arbind K. Sinha

Published for

Development and Educational Communication Unit
Indian Space Research Organisation, Ahmedabad

by

CONCEPT PUBLISHING COMPANY PVT. LTD.
NEW DELHI-110059

ISBN : 978-81-7022-056-5

Edition 2019

Published and Printed by

Concept Since 1974

Concept Publishing Company Pvt. Ltd.
A/15-16, Commercial Block, Mohan Garden,
New Delhi-110059 (INDIA)
T : +91 11 25351460, +91 11 25351794
E : publishing@conceptpub.com, *W* : www.conceptpub.com

Cataloging in Publication Data--Courtesy: D.K. Agencies (P) Ltd. <docinfo@dkagencies.com>

Seminar on "SITE" to "INSAT": Production Programmes for Women and Children (1984 : Space Applications Centre)

SITE to INSAT : challenges of production and research for women and children / edited by Binod C. Agrawal, Arbind K. Sinha.

pages cm

Reprint. Originally published: 1986.

Papers presented at the Seminar on "SITE" to "INSAT": Production Programmes for Women and Children, held at Space Applications Centre, Ahmedabad, November 26-28, 1984.

Includes bibliographical references and index.

ISBN 9788170220565

1. Television programs--India--Congresses. 2. Children's television programs--India--Congresses. 3. Television in health education--India--Congresses. 4. Satellite Instructional Television Experiment (India)--Congresses. 5. Indian National Satellite System--Congresses. I. Agrawal, Binod C., 1942- editor. II. Sinha, Arbind K., editor. III. Indian Space Research Organisation. Development and Educational Communication Unit. IV. Title.

LCC HE8700.9.I5S46 1984 | DDC 384.55440954 23

DEVELOPMENT AND EDUCATIONAL
COMMUNICATION UNIT
INDIAN SPACE RESEARCH ORGANISATION
SPACE APPLICATIONS CENTRE, AHMEDABAD

Venue : VIKRAM HALL
Date : November 26—28, 1984

PROGRAMME

26-11-84

1030-1115	: Welcome	Professor E.V. Chitnis
	: Seminar Objectives	K.S. Karnik Daniel J O'Dell
	: Inauguration	Professor Yash Pal
	: Organizational Aspect of the Seminar	Binod C. Agrawal
1115-1130	: TEA	
1130-1330	: Key Issues	Professor E.V. Chitnis
	: Production Issues	K. Vishwanath
	: Management Issues	K.S. Karnik
	: Utilization Issues	B.S. Bhatia
	: Research Issues	Binod C. Agrawal
1330-1430	: LUNCH	
1430-1730	: Sub-group Meeting	(a) Production (b) Management (c) Research
1830-2000	: Barbara Kolucki's presentation on Children's Programme	

27-11-84

1000-1115 : Group meeting

1115-1130 : TEA

1130-1300 : Group meeting (Contd.)

1300-1430 : LUNCH

1430-1530 : Group meeting (Contd.)

1530-1545 : TEA

1545-1730 : Joint meeting of all Groups

28-11-84

1000-1115 : Group meeting

1115-1130 : TEA

1130-1300 : Group meeting (Contd.)

1300-1430 : LUNCH

1430-1700 : Concluding session for Joint Recommendations

CONTENTS

Programme v

Introduction 1

Inaugural Speech – **Yash Pal** 6

Welcome Address – **E.V. Chitnis** 12

RESEARCH

From SITE to INSAT—**Mira B. Aghi** 19

A Decade of Communication Research : Some Reflections for the Future—**Binod C. Agrawal** 25

Status of Health Care Delivery Service in Karnataka : A Case for Planned Intervention through Communication—**P. Bhaskaran** 32

Indian Television and Rural Children —**J.K. Doshi** 42

SITE Experience : Some Suggestions—**K.E. Eapen** 47

Universalization and Vocationalization of Education —**Kuldip Kumar** 56

Some Reflections on Research : The SITE Experiences in Karnataka —**Leela Rao** 62

SITE was a Good Experience but Towards What ? —**Arbind K. Sinha** 66

PRODUCTION

Four SITE Stories for the INSAT Producer —**Jahnu Barua** 75

SITE Experience : Questions and Lessons : A Personal View—**Anju Daswani** 81

Women's and Children's Programmes :Need for Systematic Planning—**Gopal Gupta** 86

Portrayal of Women in India : A View Point —**Dinaz Kalwachwala** 89

The Role of Television in the Shaping of a Secular and Participative Consciousness Among the Nation's Young — **Chandita Mukherjee** 98

Strategy for Making Video Programme Packages on Health, Nutrition and Family Welfare for Transmission as well as non-Transmission use—**V.N. Raina** 103

From SITE to INSAT—**G.D. Shukul** 109

Programme Production for Children --**K. Vishwanath** 116

Television for Women—Experiences from SITE and Post-SITE—**Neeraja Vohra** and **S.V.S. Chowdhary** 121

MANAGEMENT AND UTILISATION

Experiences of Radio Workshop on Maternal and Child-care in the Southern States—**T.P. Balagopalan** 127

TV, Women and Children—Some Thoughts —**B.S. Bhatia** 132

Programme Production for Children : Some Management Issues—**Kiran Karnik** 137

INSAT Experiences : Candid Scenes from Andhra Pradesh—**B.S.S. Rao** and **B.V. Sharma** 139

Rural India is not in the Picture —**J.S. Srivastava** 151

Recommendations 156

Plan of Action 160

List of Participants 162

Group Distribution 166

Index 167

INTRODUCTION

THE GERM of the idea to organise a seminar to discuss topics related to women and children based on SITE experiences first took shape at an informal meeting in Prof. E.V. Chitnis's Office. Prof. Chitnis suggested that those who had worked on the production, research, and planning aspects of SITE should be invited and they should collectively think, as to how their SITE experiences would help plan programmes for women and children in the Indian National Satellite (INSAT) transmission system. This idea was mutually appreciated and accordingly it was agreed to host such a seminar in Ahmedabad, this being the birth-place of SITE.

In operational terms this was conceived as an ISRO-UNICEF joint seminar in which UNICEF agreed to provide incremental cost, whereas the logistic responsibility was that of ISRO. In mid 1984 we started formulating our ideas and finalised the list of participants and invitations were sent to all the old SITE workers who had contributed to its completion. The invitation was in the form of a personal note urging old friends to come and attend the conference. A part of the letter is quoted below to give the flavour of the concern that was voiced for getting together.

"More than eight years have passed since we completed SITE. One of the outcomes of SITE has been INSAT television operational system in the country. With the advent of INSAT more than 70 per cent of the country's population is being covered by TV signals. You will recall that during SITE, we had a separate time slot for school children in the morning. For women, we had special programmes in the evenings. In SITE continuity phase a similar programme plan is being followed.

In retrospect, many of us have examined how far our original assumptions hold valid in the present context.

Several of us have also reanalysed the research studies that we had conducted during SITE. Few of us have tried to go beyond our data base and have tried to recapitulate our personal experiences to ask ourselves whether SITE experiences could provide some perspective and plans that can be utilised in the future satellite systems. For the past one year, we have been thinking whether it would be possible for us to get together in our SITE niche at SAC to reflect about the relevance and usefulness of our SITE experiences for the appropriate future utilization of INSAT television system. We think, it would be an excellent idea as it would give us an opportunity to put our heads together once again towards a National endeavour."

It was heart warming to receive positive replies from former colleagues who had by now spread to all parts of the country. Except for a few who were abroad, almost everyone agreed to come and spend three days from November 26-29, 1984 at Ahmedabad and also graciously agreed to bring with them a short paper focusing on the main theme of the seminar. Due to a number of unavoidable circumstances and the pre-engagements of Prof. E.V. Chitnis and Prof. Yash Pal, the original seminar dates of October 29-31, 1984, had had to be postponed. We personally felt glad, as this change ensured the participation of Prof. E.V. Chitnis who was one of the chief architects of SITE and Prof. Yash Pal under whose able leadership we were inspired to work and to complete SITE.

At Vikram Hall (the venue of the seminar), on a pleasant winter morning of November 26, 1984, Prof. E.V. Chitnis welcomed the participants, who included not only the old SITE co-workers but also UNICEF participants and a group of young social researchers who had started working on SITE continuity research. While doing so, Prof. Chitnis traced the evolution of SITE. He was also emphatic in pointing out that some of the issues related to community television conceived during SITE are still valid and should be examined in great detail if one wishes to use INSAT for the education and development of women and children. Prof. Yash Pal inaugurated the seminar. In his inaugural address, he discussed about "cunning alliance" as a part of the strategy for meaningful use of INSAT television for the education and development of women and children. The remaining morning was utilised for reading individual papers and notes distributed in the seminar.

The issue raising session was chaired by Prof. E.V. Chitnis who broadly indicated the main areas of concern for appropriate use of INSAT television system. Mr. K. Viswanath gave a television presentation on the major issues related to television production. After the television presentation, he raised several questions about the "team mode of production" and difficulties in such productions for children. Mr. K.S. Karnik primarily focused on management issues beginning from the desirability of having dedicated production facilities for children's programmes. He also emphasised the need to shift the focus of the programme production for pre-school children. Mr. B.S. Bhatia raised broad issues of utilization both for women and children who according to him are large in number and are dedicated television viewers. While discussing communication research related to SITE, Dr. Binod C. Agrawal highlighted the positive contributions made by the researchers in the "team mode of production" alongwith the weaker areas of research. The presentations were followed by an open discussion.

A special evening session was arranged for Barbara Kolucki, a producer of Children's Television Workshop (CTW). She made a presentation of the CTW method of programme production and showed several programmes. She also discussed how special efforts were made to produce television programmes for handicapped children in CTW. Her presentation was followed by discussions and comparison between what was done during SITE and what was common between SITE and CTW production process.

The three major issues that were discussed on first day were further discussed on the second. Accordingly, three groups were set up to discuss these issues in the light of their own experiences and the written papers that were provided to individual participants. Each group consisted of producers, researchers, managers and UNICEF officials. A list of the three groups is enclosed in Appendix-II; each group had a chairperson and rapporteur for documenting the main issues raised in the group. While these groups worked independently of each other, some participants went around spending time in each group. At the end of the day, each group reported as to what were the main concerns in their respective groups. Some of the common recommendations and concerns were discussed in a large group meeting and based on the presentations and discussion, a series of recommendations were formulated for further discussion. In this process the authors of the individual papers brought out some of their salient recommendations and shared their experiences in a fairly familiar and congenial environment. Heated discussions, polite suggestions and laughter echoed off the walls of Vikram Hall. In more than one ways it was reminiscent of what happened during SITE. It was remarkable that some of the participants were still holding their ideas firmly for innovative production and arguing vehemently for experimentation and for adopting non-traditional path of production. There was no disagreement about the ultimate goal and on the 'Credo' that must be followed to achieve such a goal for the development of women and children. Outside Vikram Hall smaller groups were heard saying "we know how to do it, why are we not doing it". The "team mode of production" was an accepted thing but still there were complaints about non-availability or inadequate availability of research support for good production. On November 28, 1984, group meetings continued, in which recommendations and plan of actions were discussed. In the final session all the participants met in the plenary session in which individuals and institutions were asked as to what they would like to contribute towards achieving of the goal for programmes for women and children. During this session, all the recommendations were read out and were reformulated in the light of discussions and then were accepted by the group. It was recommended by the group that separate, dedicated production teams for children's programmes should be created so as to ensure continuity and accumulation of experiences. These programmes should be audience, area and language specific. It was further felt that greater "non-broadcast" use of video should be made and serious efforts should be made for "community viewing as a means of ensuring access to the medium for all". The equally urgent problem of maintenance and operation of these sets must also be tackled on an immediate basis. In this area of research, an annotated bibliography of video/film was suggested. Keeping in view the lack of trained research personnel to work in the "team mode of production", training of researchers and alternate methods of research were suggested. The group also recommended that efforts should be made for promoting "organisational creativity". Details of these recommendations can be found on the chapter devoted to recommendations, which was followed by plan of action.

The seminar was meaningful in several ways. It opened up new possibilities for collaborative work between ISRO-UNICEF, individuals, non-governmental organisations, and voluntary organisation. It also helped in providing a direction for the production of children's television in India. The papers and recommendations presented in this volume are categorised into three broad categories namely research, production, and management and utilization. Our effort while editing the volume has been to keep the original thoughts intact and so only minor stylistic changes have been made. With the exception of two papers which were reduced from their original, all of them have been kept in their original style. The papers of Prof. Chitnis and Prof. Yash Pal have been prepared from the tapes, taking a great deal of liberty for catching the essence of what they said during the seminar as they had made verbal presentations. We hope we have to the best of our ability, accurately caught the essence of their ideas. If there are any lapses they ought to be considered an error of judgement on our part. We hope this volume will be more than a historical document, stimulating to those who are committed to meaningful production of programmes for women and children.

INAUGURAL ADDRESS OF PROFESSOR YASH PAL

"I DON'T think any country in history has been in a situation like India's—both in terms of problems and in terms of challenges and the possibilities of meeting those challenges. Talents, capabilities and problems put together are of a kind that haven't existed anywhere."

"Messages cannot be in isolation"

".. continuous learning in a different plane is needed everywhere..."

These were some of the focal points put forward by Professor Yash Pal, in his inaugural address at the ISRO-UNICEF seminar on "SITE to INSAT : Production of Programmes fo Women and Children" at Space Applications Centre, Ahmedabad, in November 1984.

Prof. Yash Pal, the then Director, Space Applications Centre, Ahmedabad, now Secretary, Ministry of Science and Technology, Government of India, spoke of "the perspective of time scale" one gets by "substracting 1965 from 1990—25 Years, a human's working life time, essentially" and made an assessment of dreams that are simplistic and those that resulted in "other vistas opening which [one] did not imagine existed, that new challenges come and at a personal level, just being involved brings a fulfilment which has meaning."

New image for Indian TV

"I don't want just another good television system, of the kind that exists in many places - I want something else", stressed Prof. Yash Pal. "Sometimes I wonder whether it would have been better if we had no image of what TV is... If we had just started here and nobody else had TV... the fact of so many people having seen TV programmes enforces an image [of TV] which stands ultimately to be relatively uniform the world over. And that is what one is fighting with." Indian TV should cater to needs that are peculiar to India and its people. "We don't have any patterns existing elsewhere which we can incorporate... we have to go in a direction where communication, telecommunication, broadcasting, education extension, school education – all has to form one interacting mix." "So this image of TV – NBC, CBS, ABC, BBC and so on" has to be changed." "But we need to transform it much faster. If we begin to work in that direction then it has meaning."

He touched upon the debatable issue of whether one should have advertisements or not. "People will argue with you, if other TV stations can be supported by advertisements, what is wrong with advertisements ? We will be choosey. So you are choosey, – yet you have advertisements which many a times completely cancel out all the messages which you have put in your specially prepared programmes. Not only cancel out, in fact, the value orientation may be entirely different. You have no say in that. And so it is a very big enterprise."

A challenge

"Let us not think we are on to something that is very easy to do", warned Professor Pal, "... it is a very big enterprise, a challenge". He pointed out that "messages cannot be in isolation... totality counts and, I think, one has to be aware of these things." To give an example, he spoke of blood banking. "The need for blood", he said, "is about twice as much as at the moment available. A large number of people who give blood are professional donors who get paid to give blood. Still a whole lot of people think that they somehow endanger their lives, or at least give some vital part of their physical being which is not easily replenished. So the Information and Broadcasting Ministry (undertook) a massive campaign to educate the people that giving blood... does not take away anything from the body... they put Amitabh Bachchan on it with ae strong statement... But I put it to you that all this will be useless so long as every Hindi Movie goes on. The person who gives blood is considered to be a tremendous hero. He almost put his life out for somebody else. Giving just a pint of blood is considered such a tremendous sacrifice. Now this is what gets across. This is a hidden message which works entirely against you. You may make as many programmes (as you like) but so long as that one dominates, I don't think you are going to get across You cannot have just a few good programmes and hope it will make a difference".

The totality

The Prof. touched on the meaning of the phrase "science and technology for women". According to him, the people who coined that meant "working on things that will remove or reduce druggery, like the smokeless chullahs and other such devices. You may also make TV programmes on how nice it is for women to work with smokeless chullahs etc." he said. But "I would like to ask you that when you do that are you not simultaneously also emphasising the point that women are the only part of the species who are supposed to do these things ? Are we conscious of this ?"

"There are many aspects of such type which are hidden and (yet) are everywhere. So when you talk about programmes for women, can you really have programmes solely for women or children ? . . . the problem is not trivial. We have to understand how to have different levels of programming which are specific yet encompass the totality. This is a contradiction of terms but this is a challenge. The totality is what one has to keep in mind. Once all this is done and we have decided what kinds of programmes, one is still left with the problem of how to influence the totality and, furthermore, how to implement and how to organise things and so on."

Prof. Yash Pal reminisced of the programme planning stages of Kheda. "I remember there were two groups of social scientists and others", he said, "who were trying to see how to approach programming for Kheda. One group was red-blooded like those present here. The only way to do they felt, was to go out and prepare need assessment studies—identify felt needs, prepare audience profiles (regarding) number of women and children, their categories, jobs and so on. So they would come up with specific segments of target audiences, then needs, and then make programmes accordingly. They talked of the holistic aspect of life –he spoke of having man at the centre (and by man, we hope he meant man woman, and child), around man his family, his village, and his problems. So that's how one should deal with it and that's how one should enlarge it... it was a very difficult situation how to reconcile (the two) but we managed to do some tapering over of differences and ultimately came up with a very high sounding manifesto for our Kheda programme, which tried to incorporate both of these approaches in a reasonable way and one started working." And comparing those SITE days with the present INSAT ones he said, "I do believe (that if) INSAT at the moment is not quite run in an expanded version of the compact project-like activity which one had during SITE... it was a bit simplistic of us to assume that it would so run."

Cunning alliance

At this point Prof. Yash Pal spoke of another workshop they had – CREDEM : Conference on Research and Evaluation for Executive Decision-making for Education Media. "A very high powered discussion" he called it but on close scrutiny he felt, "The decision got taken because there was a chrismatic personality (who said) its to be done or, the best was, if some well-meaning people had a cunning alliance." And this cunning alliance, he said, was not so bad and that "many of the things which we made out to be very easy were also based on cunning alliance. And that is a strategy."

People were excited, he said, about the possibilities of science and technology. Not only does it enable one to reach all parts of the country but it can influence the whole value system and may be evolve a new culture. "This" he said, "has somehow or the other come to pass. The problems have changed -- they are much larger. But the other aspect (is) one is beginning to realise, one is wiser already about work done. There were questions asked and they were valid." Prof. Yash Pal was talking of rising above the definitions given to a particular job, "the way one does the work, the understanding one brings about, the total involvement of the personality one invests in the thing, does make a difference in the overall quality." To illustrate, he asked, rhetorically—"can you think of a communicator as an expert in a certain discipline—and that's all ? ; (one) who has certain ways of converting messages to a communicable form—is he essentially another version of an advertising executive who is given what has to be communicated and he puts it in a way that people will get it ; or is it more than that ? Does it mean, for example, that a communicator realises the limitations of what can be done through this but also gets involved at a deeper level ? *Is he an activist, can he be an activist* —and this question has been asked by many people who have been in and out of Kheda. Again and again, they have noticed things agonised over things, got excited and done many other things, besides just making programmes."

"Thanks to technology again... communication begins to get more and more meaning", he said, "...even in villages people have begun watching VCR's. And this is a new dimension that did not exist ten years ago. In addition, what is happening in the area of telecommunication is again fantastic... And if you were to link your broadcasting and your telecommunications with structures related to (various) aspects, (it forms) the dimensionality of the whole technical communication scene and the dimensionality of what one can do changes everyday. One changes one's agenda a little bit in terms of working to encompass other possibilities, and I think, this is the only way to go (about it). "

The active communicator

Coming back to "activism", he pointed out how useless making programmes on immunization against polio can be when children, who have been immunized, still get polio. It is not enough to make the programmes—one has to find out why and do something about it. The vaccines are supposed to remain cold for total effectiveness. Apparently "when they left they were cold, when they arrived they were cold but somewhere in between may be for a few hours, the temperature probably shot up. For the scientist and engineer, activism means making a simple device which can give the history of the temperature. What I am saying is, "he stressed that whatever we do must have all the dimensions or your messages will get effected. *Messages cannot be in isolation.*" All this was not to say he was a cynic ;

in fact, Prof. Yash Pal called himself "a tremendous enthusiast" and greatly excited by the fact that "nowhere in history have people had a chance of influencing so many living human beings... never has it happened before... we have so many varieties of people and interests which are not only different" but geographically widespread too. How are we going to get across to each of these types ? In his opinion, "there were very interesting and beautiful challenges of mixing hardware and software and many different possibilities (and) unless we stay involved in this possibility, the new configuration, which a country like ours needs will not emerge. We will have to copy configuration which is deviced for some other purpose and situation. So the challenge is fantastic."

Ending on a note of encouragement to the participants of the seminar, Prof. Yash Pal said that when he had spoken of these things to the late Prime Minister, Smt. Indira Gandhi "she did not throw up her hands, she said O.K., its an excellent idea, design it, do something, let us discuss it." Given such an encouraging leadership, it was "time to recharge batteries ; a time for renewal, renovation and enlargement."

PROF. E.V. CHITNIS' WELCOME ADDRESS

PROF. E.V. Chitnis, Director, SAC, in his welcome address at the "SITE to INSAT" conference, traced the history of the development of communication technology in India. "It is not just a procession of memories", he said "but intermingled with these memories are dreams becoming events, events becoming memories and new beings taking their place."

His journey down memory lane begins in 1962 when Indian Space Research Organisation was started, one year after the Third Five Year Plan was launched under the Prime Ministership of Pandit Jawaharlal Nehru. INCOSPAR—Indian National Committee for Space Research was created in the Department of Space with Dr. Bhabha as Chairman.

In early 1963, a Space Science Symposium was organised in Ahmedabad and Dr. Bhabha alongwith Dr. Vikram Sarabhai and Prof. E.V. Chitnis focused attention on Satellite Communication as an up-coming important field. It was important, they said, to create manpower, to train people locally who would be able to take over when practical results fructified. Even though the whole concept was still rather hazy, India joined INTELSAT as a member state.

In late 1964, Prof. Chitnis went to USA to explore the feasibilities of acquiring a satellite for use in India. At the time National Aeronautics Space Administration (NASA) had a project called Applications Technology Satellite under which they had launched five satellites, four of these were geosynchronous and the fifth ATS was an orbital satellite 6,000 Kms away from the earth surface, which could be used by our earth station. Having decided to go ahead with ATS-2, the Indian earth station was made ready by August 1967.

Meanwhile, Krishi Darshan was inaugurated in June 26, 1967. "That was our first link with television. Few read the name SITE and that was our first partnership with All India

Radio (AIR) and National Council of Educational Research and Training (NCERT)."

Also in June 1967, a joint NASA/ISRO team was created with respect to ATS-6 Satellite and the SITE experiment.

It was around this time that ideas about INSAT were getting conceptualised. It was a very small satellite with a television channel and a small VHRR (Very High Resolution Radiometer) camera for cloud cover.

With 1968 came UNISPACE with Dr Sarabhai as Chairman and the NASCOM study group was set up to deal with the software side of SITE. According to Prof. Chitnis "SITE was not an operational system, it was a learning experience. We were convinced that India should have a satellite INSAT with television communication, telephonic television and meteorology. In March 1969 an agreement was signed with NASA and in March 1970 two very important studies were conducted for INSAT-1—one with General Electric Co., and another with Hughes Aircraft. This was followed in 1971 by an ISRO-MIT study which was also a spacecraft related study. Dr. Vikram Sarabhai was associated closely with this study team and as a result of this interaction emerged not only DRS (Direct Reception System) which was there in the technical study but also the concept of LRB (Limited Rebroadcast) which is today called LPT (Low Power Transmitter) and TVR that was the idea of Pij and when SITE was formed as a project UNDP came forward with an aid of one million dollars to upgrade the earth stations and also to provide the Pij transmitter and the studio here . . . we had SITE over the horizon and the dream was coming true."

At the time our ideas in software were extremely hazy—we had no experience (but) that was the great advantage, it proved later . . . . But one thing was very clear . . . we wanted to create facilities including the studios, so that people concerned with communication would find a place to work and produce something. That was the basic idea. I must say that this has come largely true . . . ."

In 1972 there was a national symposium on space research for the next decade. The dream was to launch an Indian made INSAT with Indian made rocket and to use it for national work, development, education. Later the Prime Minister gave an indication that future communication system will be satellite based. With this there was an acceptance at national level that satellite would be part of our communication system.

In 1973 Prof. Yash Pal arrived on the scene and SAC was formed. Next came Madhuriben Shah. A tiny studio was created in Bombay. A bunch of young people just out of institutions, with no experience were set to work under a man called Mr. Vishwanath "and they all did a tremendous job". A workshop was organised by Prof. Yash Pal of people who had great interest in teaching science to children. "Managers, Producers, Communication Researchers . . . were shut up in a room till they came out with briefs." A credo was written for SITE and thus it was that the software side of SITE got underway.

"Then arose on the horizon a person without whom the SITE would not have happened the way it did and that was Shri P.V. Krishnamurthy . . . . He was the first person to accept the concept of researchers in Doordarshan. He made it possible the working together of ISRO and Doordarshan. After SITE, Doordarshan funded the SITE continuity project for the cluster areas where producers and researchers worked together. The researchers were trained by SAC and some of these worked at Pij station. Kheda was used as a communication laboratory and when INSAT came, again the responsibility for training of the people was given by Doordarshan to SAC."

"With SITE we acquired a new culture. SITE changed us tremendously" said Prof. Chitnis. It led to other experiments —"we had Satellite Telecommunications Experiments Project (STEP) and Ariane Passenger Payload Experiment (APPLE) which are intermediatory steps to INSAT. With STEP we acquired "disaster communication" and "the transportable communication" which permits one to transmit programmes from any place to the satellite and one can cover the whole network of SITE. In fact, the last one month of SITE was done through TRACT. The radio networking concept came through STEP. Also, the data communication concepts which are now a part of INSAT. Indian Remote Sensing Satellite which is yet to be launched, also utilises the same concept. "So

SITE has done many wonderful things", pointed out Prof. Chitnis.

Today we have educational programmes at University level through satellite. In a very short time, many universities joined in and others are coming forward. A couple of workshops were organised and great enthusiasm was expressed in trying to learn how to produce programmes, write scripts, etc.

Prof. Chitnis concluded his address on a note of encouragement to the people to start thinking of INSAT-III. "I rather say our dream would not be complete unless we have an INSAT of our own making launched by our own Indian rocket . . . . We have to think of INSAT-III which will be launched by our Indian rocket and then we will enter the year 2000 where hopefully our dream of development and education will come true."

RESEARCH

FROM SITE TO INSAT

Mira B. Aghi

SITE indeed was a great happening in the lives of those of us who were part of it. Logically INSAT should provide us with an opportunity to achieve salvation as SITE had only given us an occasion to kindle our soul (to use common expressions from Hindu Metaphysics). We learnt a lot from SITE, a lot which should enable us to make decisions for INSAT. SITE was a first time for India in many things, but I would be making too tall a claim if I pretend learning in all the areas. Therefore, I would humbly state, in the areas in which I worked and learnt. This was the area of science education programmes for young children (7-14) of India.

The story of television in India is a very peculiar one. Television was to be introduced in India with the objective of "reaching and teaching the people". As you will realise from this statement, TV was to have more meaning for places away from urban, affluent areas. TV was to fill the many gaps in communication which are likely to exist between people staying in cities and those residing in rural, isolated areas. But this did not happen, like in many other things where good intentions get lost due to many other overpowering and overwhelming factors. TV got introduced in urban areas and the educational objective got replaced by "television is to entertain".

Anyhow, as luck would have it, SITE came along. For a year, rural India saw the light of day—for one whole year, something so very unusual, almost miraculous, happened to the rural child in India. He got to see a moving picture which, at the same time also produced meaningful sounds in a simple looking box called the television set. This was placed in the village school. He was able to see this on a daily basis, both in the morning and evening. He did not have to pay any money for it. The world which his books and teachers in his two-room school could never present to him came to him in a very intimate way. Not only did it satisfy his long awaited information needs, but it also gave him a lot beyond that. He could see and experience so much more than he had ever expected. Television gave him information by opening new horizons. It also entertained him. Television had fulfilled the objective "reach and teach the people". All this, however, should not be taken to imply that "all was achieved ! Far from it, but it did make an interesting beginning, at least meaningful enough to guide decisions in the future.

The objective of this presentation, as I see it, is to share with you some of the learning which took place during and as a result of working with SITE children's programme and what can be its spin offs for making programmes for young children to be telecast through INSAT.

The science education programme for young children of SITE produced in SAC, ISRO Studio in Bombay deviated from the production practices of Doordarshan. They utilized a production methodology which can be termed user based. For the first time, production of children's programmes utilized techniques of formative or pre-programme research. This was done with an objective of conducting programmes which will be addressing the needs of the children not only in terms of information and research and interest but also in terms of being more meaningful to their lives, environmental and learning situations.

I will refrain from listing and discussing the various formative researches undertaken at the Bombay Studio as it does not fall within the purview of this paper. However, I shall mention the main purpose of the formative research undertaken during the production of the science education programmes. We were seeking answers to the following namely :

(1) What kind of language will be understood by the village children ?

(2) What kind of visuals will be understood and hold attention ?
(3) What format would be interesting and aid the children's comprehension of new ideas ?
(4) How much content should be put into a programme of 10 to 11 minutes duration ?
(5) How should the content be placed sequentially within the programme ?
(6) What features enhance the credibility of the presenter ?
(7) What kinds of presentations would be most effective ?
(8) What kinds of characters and setting would have the most credibility for rural children ? etc. etc.

No controlled experiments were designed to answer these questions. Quick feedback was generally required for the producers. Some studies were rough designed in advance ; for example, an investigation to answer the first question of language. A script of more than one draft was taken to the target area to determine the language level that could be understood by the majority of the children. For question 4, "How much content should be put in a programme of 10 to 11 minutes duration"—several programmes of 10 to 11 minutes duration would be taken to the target villages. Trial groups of children would view these programmes and then be asked questions of comprehension and recall. From the results a decision would be made about how much content of what difficulty level should go into a programme of 10 to 11 minutes duration.

To seek an answer to "what kind of presenter would be most effective ?", different programmes of approximately the same subject matter and format, but different kinds of presenters were shown to children. From subsequent interviews with children, it was determined what kind of presenter would be most likely to result in better comprehension and liking of the programmes. In a similar manner, quick effective solutions were sought for the other questions by repeated indepth studies employing groups of children as subjects. A continuous and consistent input was supplied to the producers on an on-going daily basis. Formative research activities dealt with the total programme from its inception to its final production and broadcast.

Some typical findings from the formative research for the SITE children's programmes are the following :

(1) The programmes were most appropriate for children above 7 years of age. Few, if any, elements were suitable for rural children below 7 years.

(2) All rural children like similar programmes. Programmes which appealed to Madhya Pradesh children also appealed to rural Dahisar near Bombay and Orissa children.

(3) A combination of interacting format with an element of familiarity seemed to work best for all rural children, regardless of region.

(4) All children responded in basically the same way to the characters or the presenters in the programme. A lively presenter with a lot of sympathy for children was preferred whether young or old, male or female.

(5) All children generally preferred a 'lie' image of the presenter on the screen rather than just the voice of a narrator, other things being equal.

(6) An imageless voice with high credibility was preferrable to image and voice when the presenter was lacking in warmth and feeling for children or had low credibility.

(7) Demonstrations and experiments were great favourities, especially those in which children were participants, giving the viewers a feeling of personal involvement.

(8) None of the children appreciated or understood heavy handed graphics and abstract symbols. Occasional use of simple but meaningful graphics especially when employed as an aid to a message already conveyed was alright.

(9) Rural children were confused and distracted by frequent use of difficult or new words and by too many complicated messages. A 10-11 minutes programme was most effective when it had no more than two new messages.

Do these findings still stand today or have they changed ?

I am afraid I have no answer to this, on a systematic basis. It has been eight long years since SITE and this long a time would have added much to our knowledge if we had continued to explore, experiment and experience. INSAT is in orbit and production centres are in existence too and formative researchers are an integral part of the centres. Yet what evidence exists today as to whether the culture of the above mentioned programme production is being carried to validate or modify the formative research findings, is anybody's guess.

As mentioned earlier on in this presentation, the answers to the questions were arrived at in a quick rough way as there was no time to organize systematic studies in formative research. The time between SITE and INSAT was plenty to have carried on this work. My sense of understanding politics is of due poverty and therefore I have no idea why it happened like this but I do have a good sense of intuition which tells me that though SITE started and culminated with such commitment and excitement, its findings, learning and relations were soon forgotten. May be we should have shouted ourselves hoarse to let the findings be known and not behaved like typical researchers, who think their job is over as soon as the piece of research is finished.

Implications for INSAT children's programme : I can only present gut feelings and give suggestions on information that has come my way from time to time.

Programmes which address the information needs of the children (like knowing about their environments, how they stay healthy, who can help them achieve in school, what is happening in the country, etc) are likely to be not only more useful and helpful but are equally likely to be enjoyed more as also enable the children to learn from them. Children can help the programme makers in determining what kinds of information will be useful for them as opposed to what the programme makers think it to be.

Programmes which address developmental objectives whether they be in the area of personality development, national integration or concept formation would have to be spread over time and produced systematically and methodically.

These objectives cannot be achieved by an attitude which is expressed by programmes spread sporadically and produced casually.

Programmes which suggest alternatives or point to solutions, arouse curiosity and promote seeking of knowledge and are likely to be more useful. Children seem ready to follow more formats, like animation and contrived situations than they were during SITE, so these should be explored.

Last but not the least, systematic research needs to be undertaken to get a fix at what TV has done to the rural children, in what way it has changed him, if at all. Has it brought any difference in his daily routines, has it modified or changed his habits of health, personal cleanliness, nutrition and the way he learns at school ? Does he communicate differently ? Has his way of interacting with his family, friends and teachers changed in any way ? etc. etc. In other words, it is important to know if we need to alter or modify our concept of the rural child. For in order to make appropriate programmes for all, we need to know him, know him as he is today, not as he was 10 years back, we want to know how he has changed in the light of changes that have occurred in his environment. I believe him to be a dynamic being so I would want to know how I should approach him now.

A DECADE OF COMMUNICATION RESEARCH : SOME REFLECTIONS FOR THE FUTURE

Binod C. Agrawal

SITE AFTER EFFECTS

PRECISELY eleven years ago, right here in Ahmedabad, in this very month, we started planning and designing for Satellite Instructional Television Experiment (SITE) Social Research and Evaluation. Today, except one person from the original research group, everyone has gone elsewhere. No matter where they are, they have been doing some communication research. This movement has opened up a new vista of communication research methods and techniques. Several anthropology departments have started offering "Communication Anthropology", a number of sociology departments have produced M.Phil and Ph.D. level theses, extension education departments have focused their attention on television, and Psychology and Education departments, alongwith child development departments, have started discussing the use of educational technology particularly television for imparting skill and knowledge to young children and students.

Several traditional journalism departments have also started communication research training. Outside the academic environment, professionals involved in agriculture, animal husbandry, family planning, health and nutrition, rural development, forestry, education, training and non-formal education all seem to be catching up with the glamour of using video technology for bringing about desirable changes. Even educators are moving forward to embrace the "new religion" of video technology for solving some of their age old problems of pedagogy. The parallel growth of Government owned television with the help of satellite technology, has made us leapfrog from a fairly information poor to a communication affluent country. These two trends are indicative of what is generally and broadly happening in the field of communication and communication research in the country. SITE in several ways was the beginning of what is happening today through Indian National Satellite (INSAT). To a large extent, the same could be said about television related communication research. Let me pick up the threads from the past to link the present and to pre-empt the future.

In the early seventies...

In 1973, the term "audience profile" and "need assessment" studies were quite foreign to several of us. Even the term pre-testing of a TV programme was only occasionally heard in the conversation of foreigners or foreign trained social scientists. It was during SITE that the notion of pretesting of programmes caught the imagination of those who were working outside SITE project. But it was still only a fashion to talk about it. The only illustration of systematic research related to pretesting available to us was from the English speaking world of "Sesame Street". Such an idea was considered premature, quite complicated, time consuming and imitative in the opinion of the creative producers whose intuitive feelings were more important than the research findings for producing good and meaningful programmes.

It was also the time when the production crew began to feel the dogmatic imposition of native researcher's thoughts, far from a keen sense of artistic appreciation, and deprived of the understanding of the fineries of production. Conflicts, clashes, propriety of positions, rights, privileges and prerogatives, all became part of the vocabulary of the producers, researchers, managers and decision makers.

Rooms were full of smoke emanating from pipes, cigars and cigarettes. It was from these naiveties and arrogance that there emerged a bit of tolerance and coexistence and, to my mind, a research tradition in communication that we had begun to recognise. It was referred to as audience research in

Doordarshan corridors, and communication research here and elsewhere in the country.

Every one of us who participated in those stormy days may have had different interpretations but those interpretations did not blur our common goal, nor the "objective reality" in which communication research as a whole has matured.

The value of communication research and evaluation as an integral element in the TV production process for planning decisions and mid-core corrections were not minimised then and cannot be underscored now.

At this juncture, I would like to raise a question to myself as to what extent have we been in a position to prove our worth as communication researchers in academics and media organizations ? Have we been able to create only jobs for the researchers in media organizations or in addition, have been able to make meaningful contributions ? When I try to find an answer to these questions, I sometimes get perturbed because we have not, in several cases, been able to make meaningful contributions to the overall improvement of the production quality or helped in achieving the goals of informing, educating, and entertaining the TV viewers. This is even more so when we look at the programmes made for half of humanity - the women. For children in SITE, we were, to some extent, able to produce quality programmes. It is in this perspective that I would like to briefly express what has been done since SITE days and what can be done in future.

Achievements

First and foremost, we have been able to create visibility and awareness among the media personnel about the usefulness of communication research in producing programmes for education and development for special target groups. Also, we have been able to enforce the idea that research can and should provide useful inputs and support for quality programme production. At an institutional level, this is clearly accepted by the very presence of the Research and Evaluation Cell in SITE continuity areas and even the newly opened television stations have Audience Research Units. A similar feature is also seen in the field of education. The result is increasing institutionalization of communication research in media and educational organizations.

The second gain has been that of fostering the team mode of production. This idea existed even before SITE and was fairly established for the production of educational and agricultural programmes. At that time the educators or the extension workers took the responsibility of acting as bridges between the subject matter specialists, producers, and the students or cultivators. During SITE, these roles were clearly defined and an additional element of communication research was incorporated in the production process. Since then the "ideal type" production team consists of producer, subject matter specialists, researcher along with script writer and production crew. This ideal type has been incorporated in almost all planning documents wherever there is a discussion on educational and developmental programme production.

In concrete terms, the production training of television personnel, as of now, includes the researcher as a member of the production team. I am not sure whether this idea of team mode of production has really been integrated into the total production process—Whether the communication researchers have really been contributing in the overall conception and realization of the production to achieve developmental goals or have they become an additional hand to the production crew or an additional name on the TV screen from among those who contributed to the final production.

Areas of concern

There are two issues that must be squarely grappled with while we are discussing the team mode of production. First, whether the communication researcher acts as a generalized consultant in the overall realization of any programme or as a specialized subject matter-cum-communication researcher who would act as a bridge between the viewer and the creative urges of the producer for realizing a programme that could be both stimulating, interesting, comprehensible and artistically satisfying.

As I see today, the tendency among the researchers is either to get completely submerged in the production maze or to take a very hardened, detached and alienated view while performing the bridging role. In either case, the role of researcher more or less, remains a supporting one—a service function, and not a leading one. I think it is this kind of conflict that I have been observing from the days of SITE till today. In the recent training programmes in which I have participated, I have had occasion to discuss these issues with the communication researchers. Many have expressed their keen desire to learn production as they feel insecure to be simply in the role of a researcher or insignificant in the production team.

During SITE, it was an experimental approach that loomed large over our minds. The over-riding consideration was that of searching new ways and means to meet both technical and social objectives of the experiment. The complexity of the experiment, its time-bound nature, its consonance with other external factors and above all a commited leadership brought diverse elements and temperaments together. Interface, accommodation, appreciation, and retrospection were accepted norms of the "work ethic". In the INSAT framework, we have moved away from experimental to an ongoing operation. In the hardware dimension, the earlier work ethic continues but in software such a work ethic is gradually vanishing as the very core of research capabilities have withered away and dissipated to accommodate other needs.

Communication research in the production process is yet to mature as it is in great short supply and the few of us who had attempted seem to be moving away. It looks like the work environment of the production system is not congenial for transplanting such a team mode of production which is under great distress. For the future, one of the optimistic silver linings for communication researchers to work in team mode of production would be to carve out specific kind of production. What I am suggesting is to move away from generalized communication research and focus our attention on specific areas for special target groups. In order to make our task meaningful, we have to leave broad diffused audience research and focus on specific target audience researches in which it would again not be enough to say children or women, but we must further break it down and ask children of what age, socio-economic class and linguistic region ? Similarly we must think of women not as a broad category but more specifically in terms of belonging to a certain socio-economic class, region, setting and education. Once we start looking in this perspective, the country starts looking more like a mosaic made up of multiple distinct social groupings and hierarchies having distinct needs and aspirations and requiring unique media treatment in order to contribute to their development. So monolithic programming could be avoided. Once a series of such researches are conducted, one can test the strengths and weaknesses of formats, topics, treatment and presentation techniques that would enable a more generalized model to be used at the regional and national level over a period of time.

Since SITE days we have been continuously discussing and trying to identify the area requiring the major research thrust. We have come a long way to recognise and emphasize, that the limited resources of research must be utilized at the formative stages and that we must avoid *post facto* audit functions as far as possible. Also we have been arguing time and again that, while formative researchers should be an integral part of the production system, it would be desirable to encourage outside agencies to take up the summative evaluation in order to maintain a high level of objectivity.

These sentiments have been echoed on several occasions and have also been accepted by the INSAT software planners. As a part of the plan, broad categories of communication researchers with special skills in subject matter areas were recommended. So far our achievements in this area has not moved beyond the demonstration stage in meetings, conferences and symposia. There is a gap between the pronouncements and practice. While holding the original contention, I think the time has come to put our ideas into practice which I think can be done only if we focus on specific target groups for research.

My colleagues have been telling me that formative research must be fairly quick and dirty as it has a limited purpose and few users. Hence, the nitty gritty and research jargons must be kept out of our work and we should be to the point, brief, and comprehensible. I have watched and occasionally participated in qualitative indepth quick and dirty research process. I have been trying to fathom how far and how much we have succeeded in this new found solace, far way from the rigorous methodology taught in the class rooms based on the traditions of empiricism and scientific objectivity. I am sad to say that in the bargain, it seems, except for a few, the majority have followed short cut methods which are not acceptable anywhere.

The steps and formats have taken over the content and systematic investigation. We started formative research from open ended schedule guides following systematic sampling techniques and moved to a "clinical approach". Over a period of time, we gave up our systematic schedules and sampling techniques in favour of clinical indepth probing. This loss led to irreparable degeneration in our findings as it was difficult for many to be good at the clinical approach. Several of us may disagree with this diagnosis but there is no denial that we have deteriorated. Probably this is the reason why grafting has not borne fruits of better quality. I think we need to research ourselves in great depth to answer this question.

A three-pronged approach to solve such a problem is essential in the present context. I think, we have to integrate communication research with a discipline based professional knowledge in an interdisciplinary framework. Such professionals, I hope, will be able to understand the needs and problems of specific target groups.

We also have to combine this with participatory research methods which will yield meaningful results for comprehending social reality. In addition, training material on research methods using first hand experiences will help evolve an indigenous research methodology. A certain amount of fundamental research related to human communication in non-operational mode will be essential as such researchers cannot be entrusted to those who are fully occupied with full time, day-to-day organizational responsibilities. This should be done in collaboration with the producer who is also free from production commitments.

These are some of my concerns that I would like to share with you for further discussion and clarification.

PLANNED INTERVENSION THROUGH COMMUNICATION

P. Bhaskaran

INTRODUCTION

ONE OF my academic pre-occupations for the last three years has been to find some practical solutions for the problems in the implementation of the health care delivery services in the rural areas of Tamil Nadu and Karnataka which include the problems in the management and administration of health, hygiene, nutrition, maternal and child health care services, etc. This has resulted in two major studies in the field of health care management.

These two studies, as we are going to see in our subsequent discussions have shown that even though more than seven long years have passed since we completed the SITE in about 2,400 villages spread over six states, yet a large majority of the rural masses in the rest of the country are still living in a shameful state of ignorance, dirt and squalor. This is because they are still untouched by the formal and non-formal system of education, mass media and all such channels of inter-personal and mass communication. In other words, there exists a wide communication gap between the intended beneficiaries of the various development schemes and the functionaries who manage these programmes. Unless the gap is bridged by carefully designed mass education campaigns, preferrably by using the audio-visual aids like films and television programmes followed by field demonstration methods and rural leadership training programmes, the functional efficiency of the systems which implement the schemes will be much less than the desired optimum. Therefore, it is needless to say that in the years to come the INSAT programmes will have a leading role to play in providing the much needed education and enlightenment to the rural masses and thereby helping them to improve the quality of their lifestyle.

In this paper I take the opportunity to spell out the needs for programmes which would help in the general improvement of health and health related services – and that too on the limited amount of information I have from the rural areas of Karnataka. The ideas presented in this paper, therefore, can at the best be considered as indicative of the need for the different kinds of programmes but in no sense exhaustive because both in terms of the content and in its geographical coverage it tries to cover only a limited area.

A case for planned intervension through communication

Like many other habits, health care is also a habit, born out of several factors, like a person's social and economic environment. Of these, one factor viz., the availability of the services at a cost they can afford, is very important. If this is the case, then one of the major functions of a Health Care delivery system operated by the government like that of ours, in addition to the preventive and curative measures provided to the beneficiaries, is to change the influence of the social and economic environment by a process of education and interpersonal and mass communication so as to help the people acquire new values. More emphasis was placed on the role of the audio-visual media, especially the films and TV programmes, the lower and the middle level functionaries such as the ANMs, Health visitors, other para-medical staff and the doctors who are employed in the hospitals and the PHCs because, as it is mentioned often, as far as the planning is concerned there is nothing seriously wrong with other approach but time and again we have failed to implement the various health and family welfare schemes and consequently, to reap the optimum benefits which could result from them. It is our contention that if there is adequate communication support to the programmes and if the health functionaries in each and every place are doing their assigned tasks or expected duties effectively then there would be a great deal of attitudinal and behavioural change among the people. Thus, one of our main attempts in this study is to verify these assumptions. In order to do this, we need some tangible evidence obtained on the basis of first hand information and hard data.

Women's age at the time of marriage among different communities

As we are all aware, the age at which women are married is an important determinent of the social change that has taken place in each community. According to the data collected from the 24 villages included in the sample, the women in this area, irrespective of their caste or community, generally marry when they are between 13 and 19 years of age.

A comparison between the villages where the PHCs or SHCs are located and those of the remote villages has indicated that the high incidents of early marriage among women were more prevalent in the group of remote villages compared to those of the SHCs and PHC villages. This finding was consistent in all the 8 PHC areas which indicated that these villages have been neglected both by the media and by the health staff in this regard.

Average number of children per women and the percentage of still births

These two questions are related to a whole host of other issues. For example, early marriage will certainly result in a greater number of child births per wompn, on an average. Frequent child birth, especially at a young age will weaken the health of the mother, and as a result, her chances of having still born babies will be greater.

According to the data obtained in this study, all these assumptions were found tenable. For example, the average number of children per women taking the entire area into consideration, were 4.3 to 5.3. This average figure in the case of the PHC and the SHC villages as 4 to 5 whereas the same in the case of the remote villages was between 5 and 6. One should remember that these figures are only averages but in certain cases the actual number even exceeded 8. One must consider the fact that compared to the villages which have

PHCs and SHCs the number of remote villages are far too many and they form almost 90 to 95 per cent of the total number of villages in the entire state. Therefore, if these villages are not given the attention due to them it will certainly result in the failure of the entire programme.

Regarding the incidents of still births during the previous year, there was considerable amount of variation in the figures from one place to the other. Data indicated that incidents of still births was higher among the remote villages (3.7%) compared to those of the SHC (2.9%) or PHC villages (3.3 %).

Details of abortion cases

According to the data, illegal abortion was practiced in most of the villages for various reasons. The only one PHC are where it was not practiced was in Kaiwara. Analysis has indicated that in 75 per cent of the PHC villages, 50 per cent of the SHC villages, and 25 per cent of the remote villages people are still going to the local quacks in order to get rid of pregnancy illegally.

The number of such abortion cases during the past one year among 21 of the 24 villages where the study was conducted, was estimated to be about 72. The number of such cases did in fact vary from place to place.

We are of the opinion that the facilities for the medical termination of pregnancy must be made available in all the PHCs to all those who need this service, irrespective of the fact that the particular women needing this service are married or single. This is because, it is not the moral issue here but a medical problem.

Mortality rate among children

In all, there were 141 cases of child mortality during the past one year in the area where the study was conducted. Out of the 24 villages in as many as 14 villages cases of child mortality were reported. Areawise deaths of children were reported from all the PHC areas.

Breast feeding practices

According to the data, in about 67 per cent of the PHC villages, SHC villages and the remote villages it was found that in 88 per cent of the first, 50 per cent of the second and 62 per cent of the third they began breast feeding three days after the child was born. The data did not indicate even a slight degree of change in the habits of the people. For example, people from all the sample villages, except a PHC village, said that giving colostrum to the babies was harmful. They therefore used to discard the colostrum. Had they been told of its benefits by the paramedical staff who were visiting these villages they certainly would not have followed their old practice.

Now-a-days, in all the PHC and SHC villages, the new born babies are given glucose water for the first three days. In addition to this, in some villages, they also give castor oil. In the case of the remote villages the practice of giving glucose water is prevalent only in 50 per cent of the sample but in about 88 per cent of them castor oil was given to the babies as their tradition demanded.

Further, it seems from the data, that the duration of breast feeding was normally two to three years because nearly in 62 per cent of the villages the people reported it and only in the remaining 38 per cent did they say that the normal duration of breast feeding was one year. Most of the villages where people said that they normally start weaning the child in about a year, belonged to the PHC villages.

Supplementary diet for children

The last question in this section was about the practice of giving supplementary food to the babies. The data in this case suggested that in as much as 92 per cent of the villages the supplementary food was given to the children only after 6 months and of which 29 per cent did so only after one year. Here again, the health functionaries and the mass media have not been fully found very useful in educating the people and thereby changing their age-old practices and beliefs.

Regarding the type of foods given to the children there was practically no difference between the food taken by the adults and those given to the children. In fact they were also given the same Ragi, Malts and Rice. Some people also had to give their children biscuits, baby foods such as Farex, Glaxo etc. and cow's milk. Of these, biscuits were said to be popular in all the villages. Farex and other baby foods were habitually used only in the PHC villages. Similarly, cow's milk was given as a supplementary food to the children in 25 per cent of the PHC and the remote villages and 38 per cent of the SHC villages.

Type of common diseases among children

The type of diseases which were reported to be found commonly among children in the area, irrespective of the fact whether a particular village belongs to the SHC, PHC or the remote village areas included fever, cough and colds. The incidents of dysentary and diarrhoea were also very common whereas scabies was reported to be found commonly only in one of the remote villages.

Treatment for diseases

The data indicated that in the whole area, except in two of the remote villages the children were taken to the PHC/SHC or other hospitals for periodic medical examinations. However, this has, in general, been done only when they had some problem. The only exceptions were Kamasamudram and Beechaganahalli villages. In about 63 per cent of the villages the doctors were available for advice.

Immunization

Among the different kinds of immunization services provided in villages, the coverage of the primary vaccination was only to the extent of 88 per cent. According to the rule, however, it should have been cent per cent. Similarly, the extent of the polio, BCG, and DPT vaccinations was still less—only in 80, 75 and 71 per cent of the villages respectively. The villages which did not get these services fully were mainly the remote ones.

Prenatal and antenatal care

People from almost all the villages (83 %) have been going to the PHC and SHCs for the periodic check-ups. The villages from where the women did not go for these periodic check-ups were all from the remote villages. Data has clearly indicated that the paramedical staff working at the lowest levels were indeed attending to their duties related to the curative aspect of service rather seriously.

Food habits during pregnancy and after child birth

An analysis in terms of PHC, SHC and remote villages has shown that in 63 per cent of the PHC villages the women ate more food during pregnancy whereas in the case of SHC and the remote villages their proportions were only 25 and 13 per cent.

The proportion of villages where the women consumed more food during the lactation period was 88 per cent, 88 per cent and 75 per cent respectively of the PHC, SHC and the remote villages.

Regarding the sources of this information the data has clearly indicated that in as much as 88 per cent of the villages this information was given to them by their elders. In addition to these elders it is said that the ANMs, LHVs and doctors also have been giving them the necessary advice.

The proportion of villages which received this advice from the doctors was only 21 per cent. This included 50 per cent of the PHC villages in the sample and 13 per cent of the SHC villages. What was noteworthy in these findings, however, is that there was not even a single remote village which received such advice from the doctors.

In short, the data has clearly indicated that in all types of villages, in the majority of cases, the elders still provide the necessary advice and information in such matters. Next came the ANMs who were followed by the LHVs and the doctors. Alas, radio, films or any other media have not even been mentioned once.

Place of child delivery

There are facilities to admit the child delivery cases in all the PHCs and SHCs but still a large number of deliveries in the villages are performed at home with the aid of the old ladies in the villages. There can be several reasons for this state of affairs which include the mere physical distance between the PHCs/SHCs and the residence of the patients, lack of beds available in the PHC, SHC at any given time, ignorance on the part of the people etc.

Regarding the details of complicated child deliveries, such cases were reported from 25 per cent of the PHC villages, 38 per cent of the SHC villages and 13 per cent of the remote ones.

Data indicates that the message of "spacing" had not reached the people in most of the villages including those where the PHCs and SHCs are located. The people in 88 per cent of the SHC villages said that the normal gap between the two child deliveries in their villages is only 1-2 years.

Periodic medical examination after delivery

According to the data only about 38 per cent of the villages reported that their women visited the PHC or SHCs for the periodic check-ups after their delivery. However, most of these villages (75%) were the PHC villages. People from 25 per cent of the SHC villages and 13 per cent of the remote villages also had gone to these places for periodic medical check-ups.

Source of drinking water

Among the 24 villages in Karnataka where the study was conducted only 8 had a regular supply of tap water. The villages which did not have this facility included all the remote villages and the SHC villages except Doddashivara. Among the PHC villages, Dibhur also did not have this facility.

In all the villages a large number of people depended on the surface wells for all their water requirements. Hardly ever are these well chlorinated.

Sewage disposal

Only in three out of 24 villages there were some facilities for the disposal of waste. In all the other places the residents themselves were supposed to do the cleaning and to make arrangements for the disposal of waste. The total number of bathrooms in proportion to the total number of houses in the area, works out to be 10 per cent. Out of these more than 50 per cent were only make-shift bathrooms. In other words, effectively only 5 per cent of the houses had bathrooms worth the name.

Disposal of human and animal waste

People in general preferred open air defacation which, from

the public health point of view, is a serious hazard. Most of the households in the area who had cattle did not have separate cattle sheds on their premises. People were victims of their attitudes which showed plainly in the readiness on their part to change their old habits and poverty was used as an excuse to continue living the way they have always lived.

Superstitions

When the people were asked why certain diseases such as small pox, chicken pox, Balagraha, etc. occurred in all the villages they said that the cause of such diseases was the displeasure of the gods and goddesses. They also believed that the "evil eye" can cause diseases, especially among children. All these clearly indicate that there is a need to educate the people in order to dispel their superstitious beliefs.

Food habits

The data regarding the food habits of the people in this area did not show any significant difference between one person and the other. Similarly, there is no difference between the food habits of the adults and the children. The whole family ate the same food throughout the year.

Regarding the consumption pattern of pulses it was observed that habitually people ate less quantities of these.

In the case of vegetables only 4 per cent of the villages in the sample reported an adequate consumption of vegetables by the inhabitants. Milk was consumed in sufficient quantities by the inhabitants of only 38 per cent of the villages. Edible oil was rarely used in 50 per cent of the villages.

They should be told of the importance of eating nutritious food. The point that needs to be emphasized in this connection is the distinction between rich food and nutritious food. This is because they can get nutritious food from the easily available local food stuffs like green leafy vegetables, pulses, fruits like papaya etc. which need not necessarily be expensive.

Methods of treatment for snakebite, dogbite, etc.

Superstitious beliefs and practices were not only restricted to the common diseases found among children but were also prevalent in other situations where even the lives of the victims were sometimes threatened. If there were complications, as a last resort they may take the patient to the hospital for treatment.

Based on these findings, therefore, it can be said that we should try to reach out to these villages and should also do more than merely distribute medicines, carry out immunization, family planning work, etc. We should concentrate more on the preventive aspect of health care which includes an enhanced and systematic communication with the masses and their education.

The user agencies and departments should conduct serious research in their respective fields of operation and spell out their real problems and programme-needs. Then only would the producers be able to think clearly and constructively about the formal content and other creative strategies of the specific programmes.

INDIAN TELEVISION AND RURAL CHILDREN

J.K. Doshi

CHILDREN were one of the most captive audiences of Satellite Instructional Television Experiment (SITE) during 1975-76 though the evening fare was largely not targeted at them. However, the Kheda TV transmission, an experiment within the larger experiment of SITE did cater to children also. This could happen because the Kheda transmission worked through the joint efforts of produce, script writers, subject matter specialists and media researchers. While SITE was a good example of how centralized telecasting could create a climate for development, Kheda amply demonstrated that any flaws or imbalance in a system could be rectified through an effective feed-back system.

In the present essay, I intend to overview the utilisation of television in our rural areas in general and for children in particular. I will also consider the suitability of TV programming and the scope for improvement.

I think the story of the growth of television in this country is fairly impressive. From twice a week educational telecasts in and around Delhi about a quarter century ago, today we have reached a stage of having transmitters practically in all major cities of our country and over 180 low power transmitters dotting the country's map. While in 1975-76, we used a satellite experimentally, today we are using it regularly and have succeeded in linking one part of the country with another. We can also pride ourselves for switching from black and white to colour. TV has also given the politicians in power access to the masses. Before ackling the central theme of this essay, I would also like to make a few remarks about TV as it is in

India.

The Indian Television, Doordarshan, is a government controlled or rather government owned medium. In spite of this, the grip of commercialism is becoming firmer day by day. Obviously, the original objectives of development and education have taken a back seat. I am quite conscious, while making this remark, that one may accuse me of having a limited view of education and development, bordering on direct instruction and propagation. My views are to the contrary. Effective education is mostly a subtle process making lot of demands on the creativity of the producer, be he an educational producer or otherwise. Creativity is still more important for producers producing programmes for children.

Let me also add rather hurriedly, that while the number of TV sets is increasing rapidly, its expansion is uneven. There are great disparities in the rural and urban spread of television. This is also true when we compare the states. Poorer the states, fewer the television sets. This phenomenon upsets the advantage of rapid expansion of owners of TV sets in cities and towns ; the situation is appalling in villages, particularly villages in economically backward states.

The limited purchasing power of a villager keeps the television set out of his reach. His best hope, is a community set. But very few TV sets in the country can really be termed as community sets as these have not been bought by the joint efforts of the community. The sets have mostly been doled out to the villagers by the government. The government also pays for their functioning and maintenance. Besides, there is always a play of politics as to who will be favoured to be the custodian of the TV set and paid for the same. The feeling of community ownership has not gone deep. It is a government show. This is why perhaps the custodian generally finds his job inadequately paid and tiring. His enthusiasm does not match that of the audience or viewers. Many instances came to our notice during SITE that even when the sets were technically working, the custodians were reluctant to operate them to the satisfaction of the viewers. Some played their sets twice a week whereas others more often stopped programmes which did not interest them.

It is difficult to resist considering some other factors which have influenced the functioning of TV sets in rural areas as these general factors also influence the viewing situation of the children. One of these factors is erratic power supply. Complete power failure and low voltage have both effected the functioning of TV in rural areas. When electricity was available for a limited time, often the dilemma for the villagers was whether to watch TV or go and irrigate their fields.

In 1975-76, during SITE, the school programmes were scheduled in the forenoon. When I recall my impressions of those days, I can say with some confidence that most teachers regularly operated the TV sets for their pupils. However, rarely was there any pre-telecast or post-telecast discussion on the programmes. Often all classes sat together to watch the programmes. In many instances the students were as much as 30-40 feet away from the TV set. This was certainly a strain on their eyes. However, since TV was a novelty, the teachers and students were enthusiastic. Occasionally rains and storms disturbed the TV antennas or made viewing a difficult exercise.

The studies conducted during SITE revealed a range of 70 to 114 students and a mean of 95 students per TV set. The audience comprised mostly of the 5 to 12 year olds. While the acceptance of TV was there, the viewing condition was not conducive. The achievement test conducted on students for general science, social studies and mother tongue revealed very little positive gains, except for the older children. What is remarkable however is that the general understanding, information seeking and the language learning of the students improved (Agrawal 1981 : 7-9).

Perhaps it would not be out of place here to consider the potential of television in training teachers in better teaching methods as the quality of teachers has great bearing on the process of learning of the students. During SITE, trainings were organized twice, the first time for twelve days and the second time for fifteen days. Though there were some problems like attendance of the teachers and the practical application of what was learned through TV, it was amply evident that with some efforts and imagination TV could be effectively used for the training of teachers. Nearly 40,000 teachers were trained through

TV during SITE.

If I am permitted to sum up my reaction to the educational use of television in the villages of India, I would venture to say that the medium is more suited for supplementing the formal class room instruction. It should not aim to be a substitute for the teacher. Through its creative application it can make learning an exciting, interesting process. A qualitative, prompt and efficient feedback from the learners as well as teachers is an absolute necessity. The training of teachers using locally available material should be periodically conducted through television.

Now I want to turn to the children who cannot afford formal education at school or who became drop-outs for one reason or another. Effort should be made to reach these children through adult programmes which serve all—men and women, young and old, rich and poor. I have already stated earlier that, though not foreseen before visualising programmes for telecast through satellite, it was very soon discovered that during the evening programmes or the so-called adult programmes, 40 to 60 per cent of the audience comprised children. Also, they were the first to assemble around the TV set and were the most stable audience. While in Kheda transmission, this information was acted upon fast, the programming from Delhi for the six states did not reflect an awareness of children's needs. This brings out the importance of close and direct communication between researchers and producers. If one considers the children's programmes that are telecast from Delhi these days one cannot help but say we have not put forward our best. Communicating with children is much more difficult and specialised. Often in these programmes the children look stiff and bored. The producer tries to force a few nods but in the process looks pathetic.

One of the reasons for the failure of these programmes is that they are not produced keeping the rural children in view. Krishi Darshan also carries very little of what can be enjoyed by children in rural areas. There is a tremendous resource of folklore in our culture which needs to be researched, grasped, digested and then to be turned into children programmes. Very little seems to be known about the world of children in rural areas by our producers and as a result they end up making stereotypes. Even the sociologists and psychologists have been shy of studying the problems of rural children.

During the concluding days of SITE, some of us could be heard advocating the need for a separate rural TV transmission system which would mainly be charged with production and transmission for rural areas. The need for an exclusive rural system is much more imminent in the face of the rapid take over of television by the commercial world. One might argue this will reduce the gap between the rural and the urban. It may be further argued that the resources generated through the advertising of consumer goods can be pooled into rural development. The argument can be further stretched that some people have vested interests in keeping the rural people backward and rooted in tradition.

The problem of rural development, particularly of children in rural areas is real and acute and hence a dogmatic approach might do more harm than good. The problem can be tackled only with vision and sympathy. Frankly, there are no shortcuts. Social scientists need to join hands with media practioners. Universal truths and regional variations co-exist. The rural scene is not static and immune to changes and development in technology. The rural child is as much entitled to the benefits of science and technology as one born in the city. But he should not be swayed with technology. A consciousness for better health and nutrition should be created but also matched with a provision for communication, health services, nutritious diet, and so on. The problem of over population should be impressed upon but not at the cost of human warmth and compassion. All this requires a delicate balancing but is essential. SITE should not remain only a drama enacted on the conducive stage of ISRO but the insights and perspectives generated by it should help us transform the challenge lying on our doorstep into a bold step into the future.

SITE EXPERIENCE : SOME SUGGESTIONS

K.E. Eapen

PAUL JULIUS Reuters' use of the carrier pigeon, to send stock price information from Brussels to Aachen, was not exactly an innovative effort—except for exploiting an existing means of communication for a purpose not tried earlier. With the advent of telecommunication transmitting information, commercial and others, quickly across distances became a reality.

In 1965, Reuters took credit for carrying news about the killing of President Lincoln, being ahead by two days of competing news agencies. A hundred years later, "Early Bird" offered the international communication system, based on the now-legendary geo-stationary idea of Arthur Clarke, that made it globally possible to witness events as they happened, cutting down traditional notions of time and space. New uses were predicted for satellite communication.

Technological possibility tickled scientists. This created resonance in potential user agencies. SITE was a fall-out from the conquest of distances by communication satellites. Few dared to warn that technological feasibility is neither the index of success nor an undisguised blessing. Platitudes spewed. The faith in the curative and rejuvenating propensities of television was reflected at a Delhi seminar on "Software Objectives of TV" organised by All India Radio (of which telecasting was a part then) during February 16-18, 1973. "Television must be utilised in the development process as an instrument of social change and national cohesion unhesitatingly upholding progressive values, and involving the community in a free dialogue. Indian television has to shun the elitist approach and consumer value systems and evolve a truly national model. Television as a support to better education should assist the teacher effectively. It should cater to both in-school and out-of-school education. A plethora of "shoulds" for which little justification, indigenous or international, existed. Pious wishes of this kind had preceded the expectations of SITE. Problems of social change, national cohesion and education were there and they needed to be solved. However, as a change of pillow is no cure for migraine, shift to newer communication technologies alone is poor panacea for age-old national illnesses.

SITE was an experiment in teaching. After nearly a decade of it there is some appreciation as to who learnt what. The hardware magicians had their lessons which got transferred to the INSAT series. The software pundits appear to be still in square one. If the so-called "radio paddy" syndrome of Thanjavur farmers have come for national applause, implications of the perception of SITE as "Radio-cinema", as another means of entertainment, still remains to be grasped by all and sundry in the decision-making chain of Doordarshan use of development. The meat of the new medium, wittingly or unwittingly, stays film-centric with its pictorial *avatar* of Vividh Bharathi.

What the occasional or regular viewers of SITE learnt is not the burden of this brief paper. What the software personnel (be they subject matter specialists, programme producers or social scientists) could have, is quite relevant now and will remain so for many years to come. The Department of Communication, Bangalore University, held a meeting of experts on SITE evaluation, April 20-22, 1977, and it was attended by representatives of all agencies—except the Planning Commission—involved with the evaluatory exercise. The declared purpose of the meeting was to review and collate available SITE studies and findings, and based on them, to suggest guidelines for implementation by policy makers and planners. The guidelines were widely circulated among men that mattered, be they ministers, bureaucrats, educationists, scholars or professionals. Like many SITE communication acts this too did not have the intended effect. As one of the advertising principles is repetition, and as the guidelines have as much relevance and validity now as they had during the immediate post-SITE years, they are repeated in the pages that follow.

While chairing a session of the ICCTR-UNICEF Delhi seminar on women, children and the media, held in September 1984, the University Grant Commission (UGC) Chairperson suggested that user agencies such as the University Grant Commission be provided with a list of recommendations that they could benefit for INSAT purposes. Many others have sought similar suggestions in recent years. Most of the 12 guidelines below deserve to be repeated and acted upon by those who are in a position to do so.

Guideline 1 : *On Policy for Future TV*

Television policy can be in terms of utilization, strategies of the physical infrastructure (i.e., T.V. network, how many TV sets and where ?), or in terms of programme production (local units, regional units, languages, etc.). It is recommended that :

(a) In view of the audio-visual nature of the medium which will have more effect on audiences, rural TV centres should be established taking into account the fact that rural audiences have limited access to other media, and that they are, by and large, illiterate, and have limited exposure to the outside world due to poor transportation and communication facilities ;

(b) Since television viewing in villages will continue to be mainly in the community viewing form for quite some time to come, top priority should be given in central and state government budgets to ensure the installation and maintenance of community TV sets in each local centres ;

(c) Programmes produced for rural TV centres should be of a localised nature, in view of the fact that the programmes of a general nature did not attract as large an audience as expected and were not very effective in terms of catering to local needs of the audience ;

(d) The major thrust of rural TV should be to reach the

under privileged sectors ;

(e) There should be proper co-ordination, both horizontal and vertical, among media, extension agencies, field publicity units and other rural development agencies ; and

(f) In order to make programmes more useful, on-the-spot guidance and effective follow-up activities (demonstrations, supply of necessary inputs etc.) should be taken up.

Guideline 2 : *On Persuading and Motivating Viewers*

In order to persuade and motivate rural masses to view TV programmes regularly, it is recommended that :

(a) Programmes should be locally and functionally relevant, based on the needs, aspirations and problems of the rural audiences ;

(b) Rural TV programmes should be in local languages and where possible, in local dialects ;

(c) There should be segmentation of programmes designed to suit specific needs and special interests of various categories of audiences, since their needs are varied. Segmentation should also be done area-wise, in cases where the programmes may not have universal appeal for the entire area of coverage. When this is done, the name of the area for which a programme is specially designed should be mentioned during the telecast, and the concerned target audience agencies informed ahead of the telecasts ;

(d) In programme production, emphasis should necessarily be on outdoor (field-based) items. Hardware should not become a constraint in producing field-based programmes. Also production units should be adequately staffed. Lack of trained personnel should not be a constraint on programme productions ;

(e) TV centres should prepare schedules in consultation with a committee consisting of local officials, experts and users. Scheduling of TV programmes have been done in an arbitrary manner so far. Scheduling of programmes for each day should be done in such a manner as to strike a proper balance between instructional, informational and entertainment programmes ; and

(f) Frequency of the same programmes or a different programme based on the same theme, should be carefully worked out after assessing audience reactions. A quick feedback is necessary to find out their viewing preference, how often the themes should be repeated and whether the same programme should be shown again. This is in view of the fact that many programmes, both informational and entertainment were repeated to such an extent that viewers were annoyed with the repetition.

Guideline 3 : *On Themes for Rural TV*

Although TV is being used for multiple purposes, for a rural TV centre, it is recommended that :

TV should cater to different aspects of rural life. Programmes on agriculture, health, nutrition, family welfare, social customs, etc., should be telecast as part of a total package for rural development, rather than in isolation for programme scheduling purposes.

Guideline 4 : *On Information Load of TV Programmes*

Studies in the Karnataka Cluster have shown that the rural audience has limited comprehension of messages. The tendency of production personnel to strictly adhere to the instruction materials of subject matter specialists was a possible contributing factor to the high information load of the programmes. It is therefore recommended that :

(a) Proper planning and coordination between various media be a prerequisite. For this purpose it is necessary to determine how TV fits into the overall development programmes, and to conduct research to decide on the components of proper media mix. Based on this, working models need to be evolved through experimentation in limited areas such as agriculture, health and education. SITE experience indicates that training programme with good supportive coordination were successful whereas others were not ;

(b) In view of the fact that the Government of India policy lays greater emphasis on non formal education, and in the light of SITE experiences for both adult and children's programmes, the main and immediate emphasis of ETV should be supportive to non-formal education programmes. If TV is to be so used, there should be a specialised infrastructure as set up for the SITE Science Programmes for children. There is need to provide pertinent information to producers in such subject areas as science, agriculture, health and other priority development areas ; and

(c) ETV in the formal structure should first concentrate on training of teachers and development of syllabus-oriented packages of programmes, consideration should be given to tools and materials accessible to children within their locale.

Guideline 6 : *On Service Facilities*

Considering the paucity of service facilities and the intended use of such facilities by the rural people, it is recommended that :

> Programmes designed on the use of certain inputs, services and facilities must be telecast, as far as possible, after assuring the availability of such inputs in the TV coverage area. Where such inputs are not available, programmes may be geared to practices for which they are necessary. However, efforts to create awareness and demand for such inputs among the masses through telecast need to be encouraged.

Guideline 7 : *On TV Care-Takers*

The role of TV care-takers should be clearly defined. In future, convenors should be selected for community viewing, keeping the following factors in mind :

(a) They should be opinion leaders ;

(b) They should be literate ; and
(c) They should have friendly relations with all segments of the community concerned.

Guideline 8 : *On Media Credibility*

Credibility of TV as a source of information was found to be high. It was also found that credibility of specific programmes (general information and agriculture) was very high compared to news. It is, therefore, recommended that :

> The production of news programmes be made a professional enterprise. All institutions engaged in communication research and training should be strengthened so that they provide specialised and quality training in the areas they handle.

Guideline 9 : *On Communication Training*

Taking into consideration the research experiences of SITE and the existing institutions available for training, there is a great and immediate need to expand training facilities at National and Regional institutions. The committee recommended that :

> Adequate physical infrastructure, including TV production facilities be made available to all training institutions. Exposure to communication process and research should form an essential part of the training given to production personnel.

Guideline 10 : *On TV Research Utilisation*

In view of the several SITE evaluation studies and related developmental communication researches, there is an urgent need for utilisation of these research findings by policy makers. It is, therefore, recommended that :

(a) Research findings reach TV centres and the concerned user agencies in time ;
(b) A national body consisting of communication researchers be formed to examine studies conducted by various agencies and make specific recommendations to

potential users such as TV centres and the Ministry of Information and Broadcasting ; and

(c) Media organisations have a processing cell to interpret research findings. (In this context it is suggested that researchers write in a popular style, avoiding use of technical jargon and statistical details, so that their findings can be easily understood and used.)

Guideline 11 : *On TV Research*

For television research to be functional, it is recommended that :

(a) It be problem-oriented and pragmatic ;
(b) It be a continuous process, preceding and succeeding production ; and
(c) It should involve as far as possible, team research, consisting of researchers, producers and user agencies.

The dilemma of satcom users is to arrive at the right media mix and to maintain the proper balance between communication systems that are already operative in a given culture and those that are becoming increasingly available to the society. The new communication environment, unlike in a past, is a creation of political will, and not the outcome of stages of development. This has to be purpose-oriented, considering the large national investments.

Technologies bring about changes in society and, therefore, policy planning calls for comprehensive coverage of both hardware and software. It demands an understanding of what folk media, print, telephone or cinema has done in the past. The question is not only one of setting up newer facilities and acquiring the ability to operate them but also one of appreciating the origins of communication technologies (the carrier pigeon, for example), their potential and limitations for social communication. The act of picking up INSAT signals, amplifying them and rebroadcasting via LPTs is no great "service" by itself to the communities covered.

A generation not a single man-made satellite circled the earth. If the infant INSAT appears to be used in an amateurish fashion, the fault is not with the satcom system. Neither film nor radio has been adequately used for purposes other than entertainment, despite all the shiboleth about their potential for modernisation. Media, new and not so new, reflects largely the ethos of the ruling elite and their class whereby mass interests get distorted and ignored. India is blessed not only with a strong centre at the expense of weak states but also by an increasingly strong metropolis-based media system at the risk of local facilities. This may be convenient and rewarding for the continued domination of the urban-based upper classes who enjoy setting up transmitters rather than mini studios in various parts of the country.

Instead of culture-oriented and need-based communication, we have technology-dictated communication efforts. Before high powered technology came, there existed conventional wisdom as exploited by a Sankaracharya or a Gandhi.

The distance between "professed"—improving the quality of life, for example, of Indian masses—and "practiced" communication culture at present, be it the private press or the public broadcasting, is glaring enough even for the blind to recognise. Who owns the media is not all that important as long as media is run professionally and in the social interest. Demands of the technological revolution and its capacity to deliver the goods remains to be founded on more exacting professional requirements, and on policy planning. These have to be rooted on an understanding of the sociology of communication and a culture of competence, plus on the political will for use of satcom for the larger social goal.

UNIVERSALIZATION AND VOCATIONALIZATION OF EDUCATION

Kuldip Kumar

EXPOSURE to the Educational scene in the rural primary schools during the SITE study provided many opportunities to observe closely the strengths and weaknesses of the television system and its utilization for educational purposes. This experience of the SITE study has been utilized in planning the training programmes to promote universalization of elementary education and vocationalization of secondary education. The salient features of these programmes are given below :

DEVELOPING AWARENESS ABOUT EDUCATIONAL AND VOCATIONAL GUIDANCE IN PRIMARY SCHOOL TEACHERS

Importance of guidance in schools has been repeatedly stressed by various Education Commissions from time to time. Due to limited financial resources and the very large number of schools involved, however, only a few schools in some of the states have been able to provide guidance services at the secondary school level. The primary schools have remained neglected completely in spite of the assertions made by the Education Commissions that guidance should begin from the very beginning of the formal schooling, and available community resources should be utilized in this context, and parental participation should be sought, especially in the earlier years.

The fast expanding communication technology, in our country, radio and television in particular, has provided a viable alternative to the traditional approach to train personnel, especially teachers, to organise guidance services at various levels of school education. To impart basic knowledge about guidance to the primary school teachers and other adults involved in the educational process of young children through mass-media, the Deptt. of Educational Psychology, Counselling & Guidance of NCERT has taken up a project to develop instructional materials on the guidance of primary school children which may be transmitted to teachers through the mass-media.

This project aims to promote developmental guidance at the primary school stage by assisting teachers in effectively meeting the developmental needs and problems of young children especially in the 6 to 11 years age-group. Assistance to teachers will be provided in the form of knowledge on the developmental needs and problems of young children and the ways and means that teachers may adopt to resolve these in the course of their day-to-day interactions with children. This knowledge on developmental guidance will be communicated to teachers through the medium of educational broadcasts or telecasts and the Journal of Primary Teacher published by the NCERT.

It is expected that the awareness about the developmental needs and problems of young children and the ways and means that could be adopted to resolve them, will prompt many a teacher to try out and experiment with the developmental guidance approach which, if adopted, will contribute to the healthier, happier, and harmonious (i.e. integrated) development of children's personality to meet the challenges of life effectively.

This may also contribute in achieving some of the psycho-educational aims of the universalization of primary education programmes, such as increasing the retentive power by making the school-learning-environment more responsive to the development of children's potentialities (including the personal-social-emotional aspects of personality).

Preparation of the guidance materials for primary school teachers will be the major focus of the present project. The required formative research and evaluation to develop need-based materials will be undertaken. A limited follow-up of the impact of the proposed assistance to teachers in the form of teachers' acceptance of the suggested strategies will also be attempted.

Target groups

Primary school teachers in rural areas of states covered by the INSAT-1B transmissions will be the main target group, as other adults who are responsible for the total development of children under their charge.

Methodology

To achieve the objective of this project the following procedure will be adopted :

(a) Children's behaviour in primary schools especially in rural areas, which require developmental guidance, will be identified in consultation with guidance and child development experts working at the primary level of education, SIEs/SCERTs, teacher educators of primary/elementary teacher training institutions, and experienced primary school teachers. Findings of available Indian and foreign research studies will also be considered in this context. A two day workshop will be organized for this purpose.

(b) Ten modules (talks) of 10 to 15 minutes will be prepared on the selected behaviour dimensions and how selected strategies/practices (developmental guidance approach) could be utilized by the primary school teacher in his/her day-to-day teaching and interaction with children for developing integrated persons.

(c) Modules prepared on selected topics will be finalised in the Expert Group Meetings.

(d) Finalised modules will be presented to a selected group of primary school teachers for their comments and field try-out. In the light of the teachers' feed back, the modules will be revised. A three-day workshop will be organised for this purpose.

(e) The field-tested modules will be released to the Journal of Primary Teachers, the All India Radio Division of Educational Broadcasts, and the Doordarshan, Division of Educational Programme, for transmission through the INSAT-1B network.

(f) A follow-up study will be taken up to find out the

impact of the strategy adopted to promote guidance in primary schools.

TRAINING OF CAREERS TEACHERS USING AVAILABLE EDUCATIONAL TECHNOLOGY

Availability of educational and vocational guidance services to youngsters, specially at the +2 stage of schooling, will go a long way to realise the objectives of vocationalization of education in the country. This will, however, require at least one teacher in each higher secondary or senior secondary school in the country who is professionally trained to carry out basic guidance functions for this purpose. Training of these teachers, in such large numbers, and within a short span of time, is feasible if the facilities of INSAT-1B, already available in many areas, are utilized for training purposes. A strategy to train careers teachers is spelt out in this proposal which aims at training careers teachers in their respective school complexes, thus reducing the training costs to the bare minimum. It may be added that this training strategy has already been approved in principle by the National Conference on Guidance Services in Schools which was held in New Delhi on September 3-4-1984.

Training strategy

The proposed training strategy is based on the asumption that the State Bureaus of Educational and Vocational Guidance, and other educational authorities at the secondary level of education in the states, will collaborate with the NCERT in organising the training of careers teachers using the available educational technology in the country, including the national TV network, radio and other audio-recording and playing facilities supplemented by the printed textual training materials and personalised tutorial facilities.

Preparation of instructional materials for the training will be the responsibility of the NCERT. In fact, much of this material has already been prepared by NCERT. Printing of instructional materials in the regional languages, if considered necessary, will however, have to be taken up by the collaborating state agencies. This will involve the printing of about 200 pages in as many copies as the number of teachers the states may like to train as careers teachers. About 40 teachers can be trained at one school centre where TV viewing and radio listening facilities are available. During these educational technology facilities which are expanding at a fast rate, the 30-day careers teachers training course can be effectively administered in about 15 days during school vacation period either in summer break or in Dussehra-Diwali break or in winter break, without effecting the normal teaching in the schools.

To implement the proposed training strategy, the requirement for one training centre to be located in a senior/higher secondary school will be (1) one tutor who will be administering the training to teachers, (2) one class room which can accommodate about 40 trainees and which has TV viewing and radio listening facilities, (3) the printed instructional materials that trainees will require during the training, and (4) audio-visual aids in the form of posters/charts and art materials to demonstrate making of "aids to guidance" by the teacher trainee at the local level. In district and other big towns in a state where schools have the above mentioned facilities, the training centre can be organized and teachers from the nearby schools can come to this training centre to take the training for becoming career teachers. It is suggested that in each collaboraing state 20 such training centres may be organised, in each vacation period in a year, thus training about $20 \times 3 \times 40 = 2{,}400$ careers teachers within a year. The number of training centres in each state may be increased or decreased depending on the required number of trained careers teachers in that state.

The training of required tutors for each training centre may be taken up by the State Bureau of Educational and Vocational Guidance with the academic assistance of NCERT wherever required. A common training programme for these tutors will have to be worked out for this purpose, and NCERT will have to do this task. The training of tutors will include (a) familiarization with the training strategy, (b) thorough acquaintance with the training materials, (c) mastery over instructions that the tutor will follow in administering the training programme to the trainees at the training centre. For this purpose a suitable teacher may have to be identified by the school principal who may have sufficient motivation for this type of work. An honorarium of Rs. 100/- may be paid to the tutor for the professional service that he may render during the training course in addition to the TA & DA admissible to him as per the state rules. The trainees may be paid DA for the duration of the training, if permissible. If the training centre is so located that other schools from where teachers are drawn are within a radius of 8 kms., then no TA may be required to be paid to the teacher trainees.

It is estimated that for the training centre the running cost of the training programme, lasting for 15 days, may not exceed Rs. 4,000/-, which works out to only Rs. 100/- per teacher.

At the NCERT level, the main cost of the training strategy will be in terms of TA and DA resource persons whose services may be given to the states for training tutors to man the training centres, and the cost involved in the production of TV and radio programmes. The CIET's collaboration will have to be sought for this purpose.

To implement the training strategy described above, a high level steering committee involving representatives of NCERT, Ministry of Education & Culture, Ministry of Information & Broadcasting, Doordarshan, AIR, and representatives of collaborating states will have to be set up to monitor the smooth functioning of the training programme.

SOME REFLECTIONS ON RESEARCH
The Site Experience in Karnataka

Leela Rao

THE EXPERIENCES of the SITE year were varied. Too much had to be done in too little a time. Looking back it seems obvious that we should have paused sometimes to wonder what was happening.

The academic approach to research prides itself on being systematic. The clarity of problem statement, the refinement of data collection tools, the precision of analysis and the logic of the results. Seen from any perspective, SITE was a challenge.

Faced with a time-bound deadline, an unfamiliar communication technology in an unfamiliar setting and the bewildering complexity of the social context, the statement of problem was perhaps the only clear understanding we had. We were aware of the information gaps that existed in the rural and urban sectors. In fact, the SITE experience, besides confirming our belief, also indicated that the information gap was widening and that there was an urgency to bridging this gap. It further highlighted the paradox that the reach of information was least where it was needed the most.

If space technology was the answer to bridging this information gap, then SITE was indeed a big step in the right direction. However, information reach is but one requirement. It is equally important that we get a clearer understanding of information processing both at individual and group level, that might eventually result in social action.

It is perhaps unrealistic to expect that a year long project would provide us with all the clues to the complex quiz of information processing. At best we could only say that there is a social context in which information processing takes place.

SITE brought home very clearly, that we needed to come to terms with a uniquely Indian and highly complex social context in the rural setting. Imported models and methods of enquiry were impractical and meaningless.

To the struggling researcher searching for the elusive 'target' audience, even the simple demographic variables of age and sex become formidable. Somehow distinctions of child, youth and adult seem meaningless when you are confronted with a fourteen year old mother of two, if at all you are able to verify the age in the first place. It seems somehow non-scientific to process the opinions and suggestions of this child mother filtered through husband or elders in the family, and subjected to the rigorous reliability tests.

The most significant part of research becomes the search for appropriate tests of significance. The question is not whether data is available. There is an abundance of it. It is just that what is available, somehow does not seem to fit into our preconceived approach of analysis. They refuse to fall neatly into the classifications of the 'dependent' and 'independent' variables and get lost in 'miscellaneous' or 'other' categories. Consequently the excitement of collecting such diverse, conflicting data is not reflected into the rather dull and lengthy final report that only talks of participant observations. Once the participation is highlighted the observation appears only as an afterthought. It is not surprising then, that with the completion of the report there is a sense of unease. After all the struggles of evolving an 'indigenous' design, the unpredictable, frustrating field work, the warmth and concern of the 'auidence' who really wanted to help, the final research findings seem to be a set of questions. Perhaps this should have been the beginning after all.

There can be no two opinions that the beginning should always be with an assessment of needs. The question begins with the task of identifying what these needs are. To truly reflect the information needs of the people, we need to evolve newer methods of measurement. Breaking information needs into compact compartments of health needs, hygiene needs, agricultural needs, and so on, is a textbook solution to the basic problem. The recipient of information is an integrated whole being for whom these varied information needs are interactive and interdependent. The concept of co-ordinated effort in content design thus means more than the get-together of the various user agencies. Not a mixture but a compounding of ideas. This is to be further translated into meaningful signs and symbols, a challenge for the communication expert and the media professional.

That research efforts should have a broader base of enquiry seems equally obvious. This must encompass communication issues as well as approaches. Concentration on "efforts" to be broadened to a search for a better understanding of "effectiveness". Information access need not necessarily result in improved ability to understand information. The focus must shift from means of communication to the content of communication.

Relevance of message does not always depend on the usefulness of information alone. The perceived utility of information is derived from a social context, in which non-media parameters assume importance. The influence of these non-media factors in the assimilation/acceptance of information has already been recognised as crucial in communication policy formulation in many countries, developed and developing. It would appear logical that we try to identify these non-media parameters that will assist in the communication planning process, be it at national or local level.

If the SITE philosophy of rural orientation is to continue, the delivery system becomes a natural target of interest. The cause of decentralised communication efforts has been much debated, to the extent of recommending a new parallel system for rural communication complete with managers, producers and researchers. Certainly the idea should be strengthened with more research data. At the same time it might be worthwhile also to explore the available communication resources in the rural sector and identify ways and means of integrating new technologies into the existing pattern of communication. Whatever the approaches, a management orientation to communication activities seems essential.

Looking through a gap of eight years, deliberations on SITE might tend to be prescriptive. However, SITE also gave a firm footing to communication research in the country and provided insights for the future of things yet to come. The research of today must imbibe this spirit of anticipation to look ahead.

SITE WAS A GOOD EXPERIENCE BUT TOWARDS WHAT ?

Arbind Sinha

YES, SATELLITE Instructional Television Experiment : SITE—a 365 days programme was an experiment—well planned and well executed. In any experiment all possible efforts are made to see the result, and in most cases one hopes for a successful result. SITE was a pilot project for Indian National Satellite System (INSAT), which the planners had conceived for using sophisticated space technology in order to gear up the pace of development, particularly in rural India. Thus, SITE, in the minds of the planners, was to be a learning experience to provide guidelines to produce good and effective programmes, to trigger and catalyse the development activity, and assess the impact. Obviously, the special target audience included women and children too.

Other than software, the hardware objective of seeing the technical capability of satellite based television system has also been met. Satellite could successfully provide direct communication access to remote parts of India where terrestrial television could not reach for want of extensive wide band micro-wave or cable network.

From SITE, we stepped into INSAT and the television signals beamed to the satellite are helping us to reach a geographical area of more than 160 transmitter range. Television programmes can be viewed by a proportionate population—urban as well as rural. But the fact remains that the common rural masses are not in a position to afford private sets and community viewing sets are the only hope for them. The elements of community TV, at the receiving end consists of the selected villages for putting community TV sets, a public building in the village, availability of domestic electrification in the building (exceptions may be for battery operated sets), and someone to take the responsibility of operating the set during transmission hours. INSAT Doordarshan plan is supposed to take care of these important elements.

Based on my continuous contact with a SITE village in north Bihar and my proximity with Kheda Communication Project as well as observation of INSAT programmes, this paper aims at presenting some of the view points of the viewers of Ismailpur (Bihar) and numerous others like them elsewhere in the country. It will try to indicate what they experienced during SITE and what they expect with INSAT. Though the discussion is valid for general viewers, the emphasis is on women and children. SITE or INSAT—any system, experimental or operational—cannot be discussed in isolation e.g. programme production or its utility and impact. The way it is planned and executed is equally significant.

One cannot forget the hard time the village selection team had in collecting feasibility data. We visited a very large number of villages scattered in the sands of Rajasthan, the forests of Orissa and the flood affected north Bihar. Utmost care was taken in selecting the SITE villages. I still remember the senior officials from Space Applications Centre, Ahmedabad, who were on their toes, to see the electrification work completed in time. Of course, it was a time bound programme. Special instructions were given to supply regular power during the TV transmission hours. Villagers on many occasions did not allow the flour mill to run for a fear that power supply to the TV may get affected.

When it came to the operational stage—INSAT—power became scarce and villages in Bihar many a times do not get power for days together. SITE tried to count the number of days TV sets did not work while INSAT counts the number of days TV really works. Custodians are apathetic. Even the well-planned, very localised Kheda Communication Project in a very progressive state like Gujarat could not ensure more than 20 per cent of the sets to be operational.

Reasons may be many. Village selection has gone into the hands of the district administration and the amount of influence working at that level is known.

TV for school children

Television has been useful in the basic learning of children. Children learning language, imitating actions, making dolls and learning about the immediate environment through TV have been reported from various SITE studies. But there had been problems in syllabus based courses and science programmes which constituted the bulk of the morning SITE telecast. Programmes were not comprehended by the lower primary children of 5-8 years of age studying in class 1-3. It was observed that science, mainly of cause and effect can be comprehended after 9 years of age (Sinha 1981). This was also because no post-telecast discussion took place in a majority of the schools (Bhaskaran 1977 : 157) which should have been done as per the original plan. The standard of teaching through television was higher than the general village school standard. Equipments for practical demonstration were not available in most of the schools. INSAT should take heed of the SITE results that programme comprehension was poor among younger students as the morning telecast of INSAT emphasises syllabus based teaching. It should also take care of the village standard and have more "out of class" type programmes. Providing a TV set for each school is a big question particularly in the rural context where a large number of schools are one room one teacher schools and many of them do not even have a pitcher for water. In the absence of these, planning for INSAT television may increase the existing gap in children's education between the TV schools and the non-TV schools.

TV for women and children

The experiences of SITE are supposed to be an input for INSAT. The five-fold development objective—to improve village agriculture, education, health, hygiene and nutrition, promote family planning, and inculcate a sense of national integration was attempted. Different studies on the social impact of SITE (Agrawal *et al.* 1977 ; Agrawal 1978 ; Sinha 1981 ; Planning Commission nd) showed that health, hygiene and nutrition was one area where there were indications of a definite gain. This is also the only major area where women gained more than men and children and adopted some of the innovations. We have already had a look at school education. Agriculture and animal husbandry look like the sole proprietory of the men. In this situation, the results of SITE in the area of health and nutrition should be emphasised and the potentials should be exploited.

In the whole development process, communication (in this case, television) has a very limited role to play i.e. giving information/message input. The micro analysis of SITE impact study (Sinha 1981) has already indicated that many ideas could not be translated into practice because of some economic, social or cultural factor. Though awareness and attitude formation are positive indicators, it has to reach the stage of adoption. Adoption is not only the apparent gain but is also a motivational factor for others. A successful adoption has a miraculous demonstration effect.

Surveys as well as case studies recorded that the villagers adopt those innovations which do not involve any additional expenditure or need little expenditure. The suggested physical inputs shoud be available in the viewer's nearby surroundings. Many a times recommendations are interpreted, adjusted, or manipulated according to local needs and availability of the things required. This is the key point for the success of any programme aiming at motivating and rural audience, particularly women. During SITE, the most popular and effective programme in the areas of health, hygiene and nutrition, which concerned women and children, was *Gharelu Ilaj* (household remedies) and *Yogabhyas* (Yogic exercises) respectively. Women talking about nutritious food, vitamins, and taking preventive measures against hookworm, and children taking bath in clean water and talking about general cleanliness are pointers to the success of the instructional objective of SITE. The beneficiaries are women and children.

In a situation where nothing more than information input could be provided, INSAT should exploit those areas where only information input can help rather than interviewing experts on different subjects (may be health, hygiene and nutrition) who most of the time suggest consulting the local officials which the rural viewers cannot really afford. Experts or high officials are not characters the rural audience is well acquainted with and it leads to the question of credibility, effecting the total impact of the programme. What emerges is that the trustworthiness of television could directly benefit the viewer without intermediate human medium where credibility is low and there is a built-in distrust from past experiences.

After the INSAT telecast is over, late in the night my mind goes back to the rural audience. I just do not see any co-relation between what they like, need and want, and what is being offered to them. You all know very well what dominates the news-political affairs. Television has become a news-cum-entertainment medium for them. The whole exercise of development communication which we did for SITE or Kheda Communication Project has gone. May be, it is because the regional programme production centres are not yet ready to take up the responsibility. But definitely there seems to be a shift in the whole philosophy of the medium. Strategy has changed and the emphasis is quite different. The development medium is becoming more and more an urban news-advertisement-entertainment medium.

It has also become commercial. Entertainment programmes attract a larger audience. It was always so. Films produced by Children's Film Society used to attract a large audience during SITE. Of course, they also put aids which aim at the welfare of women. Now, the rich housewives need not waste time in preparing "nutritious food". Here is "MAGGI-TWO MINUTES NOODLE". To reduce women's drudgery in stove operation and cooking you have a whole range of NIKY TASHA plates which you see every time you watch a feature film on TV or other "entertainment" programmes. Whom are we trying to develop – common masses? the affluents? or the manufacturers? I sincerely wish this valuable time could be utilised for giving ideas to the rural women about how to prepare nutritious food out of maize, jowar, wheat or how to build smokeless chulla from earthen pots and country tiles.

If INSAT aims at developing our rural masses, a different strategy has to be followed taking into account the SITE results, particularly the areas where communication alone has helped.

Reference Cited

Agrawal, Binod C. *et al.*
1977 *Social Impact of SITE on Adults.* Bangalore : Indian Space Research Organisation (2 Volumes).

Agrawal, Binod C.
1978 *Television Comes to Village : An Evaluation of SITE.* Bangalore : Indian Space Research Organisation.

Bhaskaran, P.
1977 *SITE for Children : Morning Feedback.* Ahmedabad : Space Applications Centre.

Sinha, Arbind K.
1981 *Role of Mass Media in Rural Development : A Study of Village Communication in Bihar.* Unpublished Ph.D. Thesis, Vikram University, Ujjain.

Planning Commission
nd Satellite Instructional Television Experiment : An Evaluation of its Social Impact, New Delhi.

PRODUCTION

FOUR SITE STORIES FOR THE INSAT PRODUCER

Jahnu Barua

IT WAS the summer of 1975. I had just stepped out of FTII with visions of taking Bombay by storm with my earth-shaking ideas.

Like all other idealistic FTII film-makers too wanted to change the world... "to do something"... "to show something" ...in short "to use the media for development".

Space Applications Centre was the first organisation to realise my great potential. I was posted at Bombay SITE studio and given the title of producer—producer of science programme under SITE for village school children. Of the first few weeks at the studio, I remember very vividly my sense of unease before a new medium. Before I got my bearings, I had to grapple with such jargon as "briefs, target audience, formative research and so on "—all this in the midst of the flurry of activity. We were asked to PRODUCE, PRODUCE and PRODUCE cause the entire project was way behind schedule. Thus began my SITE days. 2 years at SITE and the results were 50 odd science programmes. Looking back I do not know whether these programmes have "educated" the target audience. But I *do* know of my own personal growth during these two years. By the time I left i.e. in 1977, I had gained an incredible amount of experience producing these TV lessons and travelling with them to the remote villages of India.

Since then I have been literally out of SITE. I know very little of the development at SAC after I left and therefore what I wish to share with you are informal anecdotes from my stint as a producer. I want to tell you four SITE stories that I hope the INSAT producer may find useful.

First story

The *first story* is of my very first programme. I was asked to choose a subject from the "BRIEFS" and my instant choice was "MAPS". For lessons through the "IDIOT BOX" being a form of one-way communication and SCIENCE being their subject matter, my biggest problem was the "APPROACH". The brief research guidelines, my own interaction with colleagues —all had something positive to say about using a story line, of using a dramatic opening to grab audience attention. So I decided on a dramatic opening for the programme.

"...A villager has to go to the next village to meet his relatives. He gets lost on the way—takes out a crude map bearing landmarks and helps himself to find his destination..." – Here was an opening that stated the importance of a map in our lives i.e the subject matter.

The programme was made—previewed for all of us who viewed it ; the programme worked. I was congratulated. I was thrilled. In my enthusiasm I made 6 more programmes that month—all using the *SAME APPROACH* i.e. "give the importance of the subject matter through a dramatic opening and then go into its details through various other forms .." I also received feedback from the research department—it was quite encouraging. However, it was not enough to satisfy some of us troublesome producers. We asked to take our programmes ourselves, to select villages, to screen them and talk to the children ourselves—to test first hand what worked and what did not.

My highly dramatic opening did not get any reaction – which villager uses a crude map showing landmarks ? He goes by the sun, or he stops and asks a passerby. No villager gets lost in the way I had shown. My dramatic opening was not related to the real experience of a villager. Though highly praised by the development communicators, it fell FLAT—in front of the target audience. I was disappointed.

The village child has a different notion of drama. This getting lost business has no great dramatic possibilities for him. He leads, to put it very crudely, a highly dramatic life—close to the rhythms of life and death and the seasons, close to loss and pain, fear and passion, close to highly dramatic folk forms to which he is related. He is not excited by a villager getting lost in the next village. That is not enough to grab his attention and sustain it through the length of the programme.

Lessons

1. Know the target audience not from the statistics about him but by studying his experiences about life and environment.
2. Use drama (if required) that is related to the target audience.
3. To grab attention, use device that overpowers the experiences of the target audience.
4. Pre-transmission feed back on the programme should be made available to the producer by the Research Department as early as possible so that the same could be useful in the making of his next programme.

Story two

I came back and made the programme on LEVERS. In this there was no introduction of the subject matter as a lead into the main body of the programme.

Here I present a story of a primitive family living in a cave. Completely pre-occupied by survival, there is conflict and one member of the family is thrown out. Where will he go ? Where will he spend the night ? And to make matters worse, it starts raining. For the first time, the exiled man thinks of a shelter, an artificial shelter, a roof over his head to protect him from the rain. So he builds a roof and finally is ready to sleep. But there is a huge rock in the centre that has to be removed if he wants to lie down.

He tries to remove the rock with his hands. He does not succeed. And then, by sheer accident he manages to move the rock with his stick. He used the stick as a lever.

Thus step by step, one problem after another, very logically, first the rain and then the roof, the rock, the audience is simply and slowly introduced to the concept of a lever. The programme ends here with a few repetitions of lever in its use without dealing with types of levers etc. as outlined in the brief.

We went to the village again and got the programme screened for the target audience. The programme worked tremendously. I was happy when I got a very good response from the target audience.

Lessons

1. Give the producer the freedom to interpret the brief—let the brief serve as a mere guideline. Do not demand from the producer a rigid adherence to the brief.
2. Given the length of the programme, given the expectations of the target audience from the TV experience and given the producer's own sense of programming, I thought it was sufficient to give the target audience just a CLUE, just a beginning of the story of levers. If I had aroused their interest adequately and given them the concept of lever, I considered my job done. Then they could find out more about levers on their own.
3. It is not necessary to introduce the subject matter in the first half of the programme. The first half of the programme should be devoted to grabbing the target audiences attention and for keeping it alive with powerful materials that overpower his experiences and imagination.

Story three

It was a very remote village near Sambalpur in Orissa where the TV set was installed at the Sarpanch's house since there was no school house. The school was being run under a big banian tree. I happened to visit the village thrice on three consecutive days.

I tried to make friends with the children of the village. I was particularly attracted to a "lame boy" (about 9 years old) who according to his teacher was the dullest of all because he would not respond to his teacher.

The first day I failed—the boy refused to talk. The second day he agreed to talk for which I had to use chocolates and puzzles. I noticed that more than the chocolates he was interested in the puzzles. Finally we were friends on the third day and I spent a full hour with him and I realised that his teacher was wrong. The boy was sufficiently bright. I wanted to test his sense of distance, time, space, height etc. He asked me

"How far is Bombay ?" "About 1,000 miles" I said. His reaction was casual. But when I made him compare this "1,000 miles" with the maximum distance that he had experienced i.e. from his village to the sunday bazaar (about 2 miles), he became silent for a moment and then reacted . . . "Itnaa doooooooooor . . . " (It is sooooooooo far . . . !!). I realised he had got a sense of distance.

Then I asked him to find out the number of days he would take to reach Bombay by walking. He rightly calculated it to be 500 days, but he expressed it very casually. But when I made him again "compare" this "500 days" with the concept of "year" and his own "age", he was shocked and he was aware of "TIME".

Lessons

1. The device of comparison works well. Mere statement of figures like "1,000 miles", "500 days" is not enough to give the target audience a real perception of TIME and SPACE.
2. Two way communication gets results. This is possible to some extent even on the IDIOT BOX.
3. For researchers the importance of establishing RAPPORT, though it sounds simplistic, is vital for any finding of significance to emerge e.g. it took me 3 days and some tricks to get the boy to "talk" to me, to open up, to reveal his intelligence. Most likely the boy would have had very little opportunity/motivation *to make a worthwhile contribution.*

Notes and caution

1. There is a vast difference between a rural Indian child and a rural American child.
2. The difference between an Urban Indian child and a rural Indian child is very vast in comparison with the one between an urban American child and a rural American child.

Story four (Something on women)

We are made to believe that women open up to women interviewers. My experience has showed this to be a myth.

Women relate in different ways to female and male interviewers and it is imperative for *both* male and female interviewers to talk to them. During SITE we interviewed many rural women and we found the example like the following one was very common.

"Do you go to see films ?" Her usual answer to my female colleague was "We do not get time". But when I asked her, the answer was different. She said, "Kahan jaane dete hein ii". In the first she merely gives the reason, while she protests in the second answer.

Lesson

True, to women researchers, they may give MORE DETAILS because they find it easier to solicit the sympathy of the same sex, but to a male interviewer, the women may say less, but her looks and her body language give an altogether different message—the message is invariably of protest, of complaint against a male dominated environment.

If I were to gather these 4 stories into a conclusion, I would say that the producer needs to—

(a) be involved in the research,
(b) visit the target audience in his environment before making the programme,
(c) have sufficient time to do the above, and then
(d) decide on a FORMAT based on his findings and not on an already prepared "brief".

For practical reasons it might therefore make sense for a PRODUCER to be allotted a series of programmes for a particular region. The producer *needs to call the shots* and not be *demanded* right from the beginning, so that he is not handed a readymade brief, but works closely with others participating in all the "leg work", so that he has got the picture when he finally calls the shots.

SITE EXPERIENCE : QUESTIONS AND LESSONS—A PERSONAL VIEW

Anju Daswani

MY INTENTION here is not to write a formal paper but to share certain experiences, and derive some conclusions, however subjective. Everything I have to say here is in the context of working on studio-based programmes at Bombay SITE studio between 1974 and 1976.

I joined the Bombay SITE studio as a Production Assistant around the same time the studio started functioning officially. There was much excitement in the air ; the kind that prevails when you expect something unpredictable, something new to happen ! However, the production output (if I remember correctly) averaged three to four programmes a month. We (the Producers, Production Assistants and Script-writers) were groping in darkness. TV in India was then in its infancy, and most of us were freshers, either from FTII or one of the two communications institutes in Bombay—The Sophia Polytechnique and the Xavier Institute of Communications. The only two bright spots were—"THE BOOK OF BRIEFS" (our Bible in those days) and "THE SCIENCE CONSULTANT". The researcher came in, but much later.

The first series I worked on was entitled, "Our Universe". The objective was to tell children between the ages of 5 and 7 about our solar system. The aim of the programme was to introduce the sun, moon and earth and not to offer any scientific explanations of why ? and how ?, which was to be tackled later in the series, as per the brief. The producer thought of a central figure in the programme, one who is (I quote) "A chemist or a magician who lives in isolation, away from the main community, and attracts the attention of a bright seven year old. This child manages to sneak into the magician's house/lab and on sighting a telescope, peeps through it. The magician catches him, threatens to beat him up, then turns into a friend and shows him the moon and the planets through the telescope." I am quite sure that programme never went into a transmission capsule. In fact, we did some kind of pretesting with the local municipal school children, and the results were disastrous.

I LEARNED LESSON NUMBER ONE

When you teach children science, the presentor or source of learning must be a credible figure. Incorporating fantasy into the format of a science programme may make the programme interesting, but is likely to confuse very young children.

In the earlier days of production planning, some obviously well-meaning friends had seen/heard of Sesame Street, and talked about it with a certain amount of awe and respect. Inspired by these discussions, one of the producers made a programme which presented the concept of counting from one to ten through a song composed to a catchy tune. For the visuals, graphic animation was used. An exciting experiment no doubt, for those of us who worked on this programme, targeted for children of pre-school age. But how often do you need to repeat a programme of this kind, to unable tiny tots to recall an entire song ?

LESSON NUMBER TWO

Programmes about complex concepts need to be retelecast at regular intervals. Of course, we had no means to ensure that the same children were present during repeat telecasts.

Later the producer was told by the researchers that his counting song had proved to be extremely popular. What exactly does the word 'popular' mean to a communicator ?

I would like to quote here a passage from "Mediation" by Pr. Gaston Roberge, who discusses the action of media in our society :

"The famous television programme, Sesame Street, was created at an enormous cost, in the context of commercial television, and with very particular cultural aims in mind. This programme has all the features of American commercial TV, especially its manipulative action on the spectator. An indication of the influence of foreign media in India can be seen in the fact that some educators here believe that Sesame Street is an exemplary educational programme which they seek to emulate in the Indian context. It is noteworthy that Sesame Street was created in an effort to assimilate within the so-called "mainstream" of American national life, marginal and minority groups of the United States. Will satellite television in India seek to assimilate the *rural majority of the country* within *the "mainstream" of the urban minority* ?"

In the initial stage of making science education programmes all productions were studio-based. It was a whole new world of simulated huts, painted backdrops and characters dressed in dhoti-kurta and topi hired from Maganlal Dresswala. Somewhere in the back of my mind banged the thought :—"look ! the child out there in Sambalpur or Chattisgarh or wherever, is going to believe in this simulated reality, just as much as you believe in the reality of the model village often depicted in Hindi cinema, with its mascarraed and lipsticked village belles, and its clean blue water pond with shocking pink lotus flowers."

Six different regions—Karnataka, Andhra Pradesh, Bihar, Orissa, Gujarat and Rajasthan. Each with its own culture, traditions, language and geography. And my studio-village had to represent all of them and my studio-characters were to convince them of strange new concepts through a strange new medium !

Were we creating a new myth ?

The myth of "The revolution in communication media" ?

LESSON NUMBER THREE

Creating new myths while trying to depict reality is an easy trap to fall into.

Was there an alternative ?

Yes. And it came in the form of the Pij transmission and the Kheda Operation Cell.

I happened to be the only one around to have studied Gujarati and had some experience in Gujarati theatre. As a result, I got my first independent production offer. I was handed several scripts and told to go ahead with the "Chadiya" serial. This was an exciting challenge in terms of production work. Conceived as a musical programme with rhyming dialogues, the Chadiya serial consisted of six programmes each of 16-20 minutes duration. For the children to sing and dance at a stretch, without muffing the lines or missing a step was asking for a lot. Editing facility was not available to us in those days. Such a production would need many hours of rehearsing and studio-time (which was dear because by now the studio was booked almost round the clock). Also, the working space within the studio was not sufficient to accommodate six to eight artists and a twenty piece orchestra. So, we pre-recorded complete sound tracks of all six programmes, made cassette copies and rehearsed the children till they were singing the scripts backwards. Complete synchronisation of sound and visuals was what we tried to achieve, and even succeeded to a certain degree.

LESSON NUMBER FOUR

The importance of teamwork.

Till then, everybody thought the producer was "God" ! Now there was the realisation that he was but part of a team. So much depended on so many people to make a well co-ordinated programme—the cameraman had to be fast and alert, the sound recordist had to have a good ear for music, the light man had to perfect his light technique. The Production Assistant had to hold his breath for a full forty seconds while he animated the rising sun during recording. The vision mixer went beserk trying to sort out the right commands from the wrong ones given in excitement by inexperienced producers. And finally, the artistes : the slightest mistake, and we had to start all over again. The studio was cold and so were they, but the joy of having achieved something *a collective effort* showed on every face ; as much on the faces of the hardware people, as on the faces of the production group.

The TV producer shoots, directs, edits and mixes all at the same time. He is no "superman". He needs a solid team of efficient, enthusiastic, involved people, with whom he shares the applause, but not the brickbats. "Chadiya" was followed by other serials like "Jalpari" and "Garbadiyo Gattu". By this time there were questions appearing in my mind regarding the contents and presentation of these programmes, sometimes in big bold red—Is this all I could do with the supposedly revolutionary medium of communication ? I read Wilbur Scramm which was terribly depressing :

> "Most of a child's learning from television is incidental learning." "No informed person can say simply that television is bad or it is good for children. For most children, under most conditions, most television is neither particularly harmful nor particularly beneficial."

Of course, Scramm *et al.* spoke of the urban American child, and I needed some kind of feedback, some reference points within the Indian context, the SITE context. I drew a blank—nothing was available.

Later, long after I left SAC, these programmes remained with me. It was difficult to get them out of my system. There was a feeling of confusion and my questions.

Were these programmes understood ?

> Did they generate discussion among the children regarding their credibility ? situations ? characters ?
> Did fantasy viewing fulfil certain needs in growing children ? Or was it merely the passive pleasure of being entertained, through the rapidly moving, hypnotic images ?

I left SAC in 1976. In the period between 1976 and 1984 tremendous work has been done at the Ahmedabad studio for the Kheda viewers. I very strongly feel that there is a need for a systematic impact study translated into principles which a Producer can apply to his conceptual work. This will not only help future Producers, but inspire many more Khedas. Hope lies not in a single national TV network but in a dream of many such dedicated teams, spread out all over the country.

WOMEN'S AND CHILDREN'S PROGRAMMES
Need for Systematic Planning

Gopal Gupta

THE PLACE of television is in the household, hence to think of a television audience without women and children is unusual and improper. Even in a community viewing situation like an Indian village where orthodox traditional society and its rigid norms are still persisting, it has been observed that women and children form the major audience (Television in Kheda, Binod C. Agrawal and M.R. Malek 1981 and SITE Winter School-1976).

Comprehension and adoption of the messages received through television was also more in the case of women and children, more so in case of illiterate women. This was evident from the findings of various social scientist, e g. on the whole, more females than males changed or gained in health innovations (Jesudasan 1977 : 181). Both sexes and children seemed to have picked up. health ideas as a result of TV viewing (Agrawal 1978 : 161). In general, among the female frequent and occasional viewers and control group, gain score was higher compared to males. (Agrawal 1981 : 42).

In the case of children, the study conducted by Aghi (1977 : 16-38) in the schools of Rajasthan showed that TV exposure of science education programmes stimulated an interest among the experimental school children of grade III and V. According to Schramm, individual gains are always there to a varying extent.

Therefore, it becomes necessary and obligatory on the part of educationists, social scientists, media planners and media practitioners to use media in an appropriate manner so as to provide information and direction to its viewers in a manner which will help them act in positive direction to whatever minimum extent they adopt or practice.

The question arises what could be the best way out and what a women's and children's programme should contain? Prior to answering this question it would be better to state whether there should be a single programme covering women's and children's problem or we would like those programmes to be categorised as :

(i) Women's Programme : Dealing with the welfare of the women and their infant children as a whole. This could be further sub-divided as dealing with—
   (a) personal health hygiene problem including nutrition etc.
   (b) household problems including care of the husband,
   (c) economic and social problems,
   (d) motivational cum awareness aspect,
   (e) motherhood and care of the child etc.

(ii) Common programme for women and children. This would deal with the training and education of the child at pre-nursery and post-nursery stage including health and nutrition.

(iii) Children's programme : These programmes would be directed towards the various age group children. In the initial stages till a child reaches third standard, an enrichment type of programme which, incidentally but in a systematic way, deals with the basic operations and contents which educationists or parents desire him to know would serve a better purpose, of entertaining him as well as informing him in the right direction. After the age of 7 or so, it would be better to provide support to the child in his educational attainments. Therefore, blending of syllabus based (as far as contents are concerned) entertaining programmes and enrichment types programmes are necessary.

As the age group increases the programme format and contents will have to be changed drastically and one will have to separate course based programmes from the general awareness programmes considerably.

The basic fact which cannot and should not be ignored is that at all stages, the programme has to be planned, devised and produced with predetermined contents and objectives. Any digression from these would result in complete chaos.

Programme contents

Detailed planning at this stage is needed for the contents and area of programming at national and regional level. In almost all cases the contents may remain same as the basic needs in the larger part of the country seem to be similar, but priorities may vary from place to place depending upon various factors like existing practices, availability of resources and things etc.

Therefore regional or local programmes would take care of the regional and day-to-day needs of the women and infants.

In case of children's programme, regionalisation in terms of contents would not be necessary at all and hence planning and scripting etc. could be done centrally. The language would play an important role in case of these programmes hence the production facilities have to be augmented differently. For any developing country with limited resources, in terms of hardware as well as in terms of trained manpower, to wait till such time that training of manpower is completed would be improper.

It may also be accepted that a well produced programme communicates better than unprofessionally produced programme. Therefore, it will be better to have dedicated production centres for women's and children's programme.

With the starting of the National Network and satellite transmission, the purpose of present base production centres at Delhi, Cuttack has been lost and it would be worthwhile to augment these Centres for such assignment.

Pij experiment has given a lead to specific programming and under the present circumstances it could also be worthwhile to divert their attention to one of these areas and prepare prototype programmes and test them.

But to start with let us think of content in totality and further sub-divide it into specifics programme-wise to give a lead to the production team.

PORTRAYAL OF WOMEN IN INDIA—A VIEW POINT

Dinaz Kalwachwala

THE PURPOSE of this paper is to share with the readers some of the thoughts, experiences and the analysis that have built up over a period of the past few years of producing television programmes on women.

The foot is in the wrong boot

Like in most instances—communication media is not an exception to the fact of having a discriminating attitude towards women. With great progress being made in the industrial field in the country, the giant strides made in space technology, sending men as well as satellites into space, there is reflected a great poverty of thought with regard to the portrayal of women in our media. The trend is more towards running after illusions rather than concentrating on the real issues. But then we have hardly anyone to blame for the discriminating attitude that society holds towards women be it in the global context or in our country ; which in turn gets reinforced in various media and thus provides a safe status-quo for the system to perpetuate. One can hardly say whether this is done intentionally or more out of common habit. The question is not to find who is to be blamed but whether we are prepared to see the problem afresh.

All this seems even more alarming when one thinks in terms of a medium like television. With a transmitter-a-day strategy planned for rapid spread of the TV network all over the country, with obvious priority and stress given to the programmes on the National channels, a lack of concern in terms of proper planning, strategy and implementation with regard to programmes on women cannot but be discomforting. I say on women because I believe that programmes on issues concerning women should have an audience of both men and women, as one cannot be separated or segmented from the other ; and more so since men are as much, if not more, a part of the basic issue.

The first question that comes to my mind, and that is to be answered by persons who are involved in the decision-making for software production, is—if development (with the basic ingredients of education, information and entertainment) is our basic concern—*do* women form a part of that development ? If so, *which* section of the society (urban, rural, rich, middle-class, poor) women are we addressing ourselves to ? The third question—How do we identify these needs ? *Who* shall identify them ? Are they felt needs or are they the needs that stem from the usual distorted, cock-eyed perspective which projects and encourages women "to become better housewives by keeping their homes pretty, learn to cook the best of foods, to win the man through his stomach and take lessons in body and skin care"—thereby turning them into sophisticated slaves of the modern age ? In fact, the problems of rich or middle-class urban women are perhaps in no way less pertinent than that of their lesser privileged sisters living in the rural areas ; their being women is by itself enough to be looked at as having certain universal similarities. What goes wrong is perhaps the erroneous emphasis, the faulty focus—the foot in the wrong boot—that reflects the lack of insight in identifying the actual needs.

Do we have the will ?

Last year in August 1983, the Centre for Women's Development Studies (CWDS) Committee on the portrayal of women in the media conducted a seminar in New Delhi on "Role of Doordarshan in Women's Equality and Development". The Committee went through various aspects of the existing TV programmes on women and also how women are portrayed in programmes of a general nature and in feature films. At the end of the seminar the committee gave eighteen recommendations regarding the contents of the programmes. To quote a few

> "... (5). The existing telecasting of feature films (including in regional languages) should be reduced to once a fortnight. This is imperative because : (a) The Commercial cinema today is the prime medium through which negative and derogatory images of women in our society are both created and reinforced," ... "11 (d). Ongoing efforts by women, individually and collectively, towards constructive/progressive struggles for social and economic transformation of the status of women and of the larger society" ... and several others.

So much for all that—and when one tries to recall certain "happenings" on the screen, a few images flick through the mind at random—

Helen with her green skirt swirling to the tune of a "*garba*" with words that emphasise the need for wives to observe ""*Karvachoth*"—a fast that Indian wives keep to pray for the longevity and good health of the husband so that the wife can become and live like the dust settled at his feet (Chitrahar—a bi-weekly programme of film songs on the National Channel).

Jai Amarnath (a Hindi feature film shown on Thursday on the National Channel) shows the heroine making a hazardous trip to Mount Amarnath to ask the Gods for her husband's life without whose existence her own life is purposeless (reinforcement of the age old mythological trend to live upto the self-sacrificing and helpless images of Sati Sita, Parvati, Draupadi and Ahilya who had found meaning of their existence only by dancing to the tune of the wishes and whims of their husbands/males—the gods incarnate).

Humlog—a bi-weekly sponsored programme serial—takes up the serious and burning issue of dowry to be hastily and conveniently solved by the girl finding the romantic hero of her dreams. Alas, if only it were that simple ! Or take another instance from the same serial—Master Pritam, a singing teacher comfortably fondles his "student" who in turn takes it all without even batting an eyelid.

Jai Santoshi Ma (a Hindi feature film shown on a Sunday evening) shows the heroine being tortured, beaten, reduced to rags—all for the husband who has left her in search of wealth and has happily forgotten her—thanks to the spell cast by a group of scheming Goddesses who are playing their heavenly politics against their arch rival—Goddess Santoshi (a fictitious character). The heroine keeps a series of "Vratas" (fasts) in the name of Goddess Santoshi. The Goddess is pleased and the husband returns. The Goddess descends on earth and blesses the couple. All her troubles and miseries are over and she forgives all who had tortured her and made her unhappy. The result-scores of women in the audience started observing fasts in the name of the new Goddess Santoshi.

The other "harmless" programmes only show women enacting their stereotyped roles, that of wife, mother, daughter—the silent spectators, watching the events of their lives being written by someone else. In short, anything but individuals capable of thinking, deciding and acting as per their own wishes. It is also not that such characters do not exist in real life situations. They do—but I suppose, it is generally considered "safe" to replicate the age-old cut-out images of women that fit into and suit our so-called Cultural Heritage.

This also does not mean that there are no positive efforts. But they are so few and far between that they get lost and over-shadowed by the oft shown glamourous emulsion which wipes it all out with one giant stroke.

Some experiences

At this stage it becomes imperative to share some of the work in this regard that we have done at the Space Applications Centre for Pij television (the Kheda Communications Project). To date I have worked as a Producer/Director for four women's serials. The first one called "Jagi ne Joun To—" (If I wake up and see . . .) was produced with the objective to provide a platform for rural women to voice their thoughts, their concerns, their problems on issues that effect them e.g. the discriminating attitude between boy and girl child, the upbringing process, the decision-making process, the workload distribution, dowry, harrassment, marriage, employment, self-image of women, education, etc. Men also discussed their views about these issues since the objective was also to create a better understanding, a dialogue between men and women, besides building the self-confidence of women by creating a horizontal communication link.

It so happened that on our several field visits when we interviewed people in the villages, several stories, incidents were narrated on the same topics, both on and off camera, which we later incorporated by way of getting scripts written and enacting them in drama format.

The research feed-back indicated that the programmes were liked by both men and women. Though primarily aimed at raising opinions about women's issues, it was very heartening to see that the programmes did not antagonize the men, the proof being that we received six drama scripts based on real-life incidents from village men, two of which finally got selected and produced. This serial ran for 32 weeks with a once-a-week transmission schedule.

The second serial that I produced was *Nari-Tun-Narayani* —a 40 parts serial that set a trend for a new kind of approach ; a gratifying and a great learning experience for all of us who were involved. We had a core team of a researcher, a writer and a producer and *Nari-Tun-Narayani* became their common baby, their joint headache. The serial done in a dramatic format went a step further than just portraying "reality" as it is. For by then we felt a great need to go beyond just portrayal of problems, not by giving solutions or formulas but by suggesting certain directions. The objectives of *Nari-Tun-Narayani* were (a) to make women realize the need for being economically self-reliant and to acquire a strength of their own, (b) to realise the need to come together through a "Mahila Mandal" or otherwise, to combat their social as well as economic difficulties, (c) to also make them realise that doing so is a tough process but that one should not lose hope without making sufficient effort.

The serial focused on the need and the process that the rural women go through to form a co-operative society in the village and produce coir-products for urban as well as rural market. Introduction of various government schemes (along with their loop-holes) and the difficulties that the women face in organizing themselves were highlighted. The social problems and family resistance, with their small triumphs, their progress and certain success stories were also incorporated. The serial though performed in a dramatic format enjoyed tremendous amount of credibility and popularity amongst the audience. (A detailed report on the serial—"A retrospective look—*Nari-Tun-Narayani* has been prepared.)

After the completion of *Nari-Tun-Narayani* a silent period followed—a silence full of pregnant meaning. Our eyes shifted to the legal side. Our Indian constitution is one which is so often praised as being a brilliant document of human rights and justice – and quite rightly so. But on the other hand, the same land which guarantees such human rights, is full of small and big atrocities that a vast majority of its women inhabitants are subjected to, day in and day out. Mere knowledge about law and its protection is certainly not a guarantee that one shall attain it—but knowledge does finally go a long way in acquiring the same. Equally true is that information about legal provisions is not adequate if it is not accompanied by a perspective look at the social aspect of the problem. And this back-drop gave birth to a new idea for another serial—*Nyay-Anyay*. But before we come to *Nyay-Anyay*, I would want to refer to a very interesting, action-packed and stimulating experience we went through and that was of—*Bhadke Bale che Zindagi* (My life is in flames).

It so happened that while we were preparing and collecting our research data to launch our new serial – *Nyay-Anyay*, we came across a newspaper cutting which said that a young wife in an urban area of the city died of burn injuries from the cooking stove. The report however added, that seventeen neighbouring women have submitted a memorandum expressing their doubt about the nature of Varsha Dixit's (the victim) death and suspect it to be murder. Varsha, the report added, was the mother of two young sons. The matter caught our interest, obviously due to the unusually bold stand taken by the neighbours. I would not want to go into much details as to how we went about making the programmes, which were mainly interview-based. What is interesting was what followed.

From the four programmes that we made on Varsha Dixit's death event, the last one included the public's cry and the demonstration of nineteen women's organizations, against the undignified and partial behaviour of the police. We decided to telecast the serial on a daily basis. What followed was a series of calls, frantic running around to the courts and receiving some stay orders trying to stop further telecast of the programmes. The unflinching attitude and decisiveness shown in those tension filled days by our management personnel, made it possible for at least three programmes to go on the air. A detailed research study was conducted on the impact of these programmes in the urban as well as rural areas and the results are simply dumbfounding. What perhaps takes a series of 40-50 parts done in a dramatic form to achieve, this short serial did in just three parts. One is not trying to say that this is the best way to go about such themes but it is certainly worth trying to see how the whole socio-legal system goes topsy-turvy when real persons are involved. The strength of the medium then shows its full force.

Nyay-Anyay which is our current endeavour, has just made its beginning. We present a real life story in a drama format which is followed by a simplified version of the legal provision (given by a lawyer). The objective is to stimulate thinking and generate participatory discussions with the audience on these issues, their socio-economic and cultural aspects, the availability of legalistic solutions, their pros and cons. The themes include marriage, divorce, maintenance, custody of children, dowry, rape, eve-teasing, property, working women in organised/unorganised sector and several others.

Much has been done and quite a bit has been achieved and yet one is still left with a gnawing feeling in the heart. What can television alone do ? In a situation where the condition of women on the one hand is showing an encouraging sign of self-reliance and on the other hand where the atrocities on them are increasing—what can television do to bring about change—specially when the infrastructural facilities and the social system reflects an abyss of poverty in thought as well as action ? How do we work towards that change ?

What can be done

As someone said, "Know the prosperity of a nation from the status of its women" and I may add, its children too. If one talks about the development of women, one should not look at the problem in isolation but as an integral part of the total social, economic and political system. Women are not something to be thought about peace-meal and that holds true for the strategy that should be adopted for planning programmes on them. The answer lies in an integrated approach.

There is a need to process an overall sensitive approach while portraying women. This does not hold true for programmes produced just on women but also for all kinds of programmes/films - be they children's programmes, educational programmes, health programmes, dances, ballets, plays on different topics as well as Hindi films (shown on the TV network). This also applies to the way in which our announcers and news-readers (women) are presented—more often as decorative elements than presentable co-workers. Special efforts should be made to portray women in a realistic, progressive and positive light. The ever-suffering, dumb-headed and ineffective image should be dispensed with.

Negative images or just portraying reality is not enough. In fact, it can often be harmful. It has been observed that sheer duplication of the dark side of life can often lead to apathy—a passivity. This can be avoided by depicting the positive images or success stories of women in whatever sphere they take place. The difficulty is of finding such examples which are few and far between—so all the more need to propagate them. From past work experience I have come to the conclusion that it becomes necessary to take reality forward towards an idealism—a plausible idealism ! Reality can serve as a take-off point but unless the challenge is met, unless the struggle is established, the effort does not hold much water. There should be a concentrated effort to question and change the age-old values and images that perpetuate the status of women in the mythological, religious and social context.

A need is there to produce programmes that talk about

inoome generating schemes for women. The danger, though, in these kind of ventures is again that typical "womanly jobs" like papad-making, sewing, embroidery, pickeles, etc. are propagated. Stress should be given on non-traditional skills which can break the myth that women are suited to certain kinds of jobs only. A systematic survey of the existing schemes (Government/non Government) and presentation of the analysis and changes needed to upgrade the schemes (as we had done in the "Nari-Tun-Narayani serial) would make it more purposeful. Non-transmission use of programmes can be particularly helpful in this sphere—by way of teaching of skills through television and presenting the difficulties of the beneficiaries to the concerned decision-makers ; thereby creating a horizontal communication link.

Children need particular attention, specially when they happen to be the most faithful audience. Depiction of typical male/female roles in a variety of programmes has an everlasting and damaging effect on the mind of the growing child whose day-to-day experience already confirms what he sees on the TV screen. And the last question that emerges before us—who should produce these programmes ? Should women producers be the sole authority on the subject ? I do not think so. It can be any person—male or female—who possesses a sensitive, pragmatic and radical view-point, a person who is committed to and believes in what she/he is trying to communicate.

This calls for a new breed of Media-Practioners, a new approach, cultivating a new religiosity, which is the need of today.

THE ROLE OF TELEVISION IN THE SHAPING OF A SECULAR AND PARTICIPATIVE CONSCIOUSNESS AMONG THE NATION'S YOUNG

Chandita Mukherjee

AN ESTIMATED 40 per cent of our population today is under 16 years old, that is, some three hundred million persons. How many of these will have the privilege of passing through the formal school system, or even the benefit of access to non-formal education programmes ? Even the most optimistic estimate will still leave tens of millions of young citizens of our country in the unenviable position of being illiterate, unskilled and unemployed as they enter adulthood.

This defines the magnitude of the problem we are considering. In what follows, the terms "viewer" and "audience" will refer specifically to this section. The specific problem under discussion here is that of providing an *alternative educational system* through the national TV network and INSAT to those who have been sidelined by the existing opportunities for education.

Will this be possible ? There can be only one answer to the question. It *has* to be made possible. No nation can survive with a hundred million of its young adults facing a grim future of no employment, no useful skills, and no prospect of betterment of one's existence through legal means.

As with the design of any other educational system, we have to approach the problem systematically, and with an underlying philosophy. There is a need to define a few basic principles and guidelines which will permeate the great variety of programming that such a project will generate.

We can already see the consequences of neglecting this area. In the absence of programming specifically designed for the young, children in urban slums develop their attitudes from what they experience, what they see and hear in their environs, in the movie theatres and from existing TV. What are some of the values generated by such an environment ? To state a specific instance during the recent communal riots in Bombay, most of the men who participated in the looting and arson were slum youth in their late teens and early twenties.

The events of this past year alone point to a growing trend towards communalisation of social relations. Why is it that these young people become such ready recruits to such false solutions to their real problems ?

It should be pretty clear by now that the problem we are tackling involves millions of marginalised youths in the process of development itself. To equip them to fulfil at least their basic needs and also to provide them with a basis for a secular personal identity ; an identity which goes beyond caste/religion/region.

Of course, this is not a task that ETV can handle alone. The scenario is a much bigger one, of national development, involving all the agencies of economic and social change. But let us recognise and assert that ETV can play a strategic role in this task. What must be the content of this role ?

*ETV must build up a consciousness of national integration, which requires the systematic propagation of a secular identity.

*ETV must build up a consciousness of development as a basic right of the poor, and encourage the assertion of this right by the poor, and their initiative in the face of all economic and social obstacles.

*ETV must build a consciousness of the method of science as a habit of thought for all, including the poor and unlettered. It must build the scientific temper as an integral component of the common person's culture.

What this means is that we have to establish and work with a fresh concept of TV programming, one which concerns itself frontally with the lives and aspirations of the poor. The content of the programming as well as the forms, the method of approach must have complete credibility with its audience. Only then can it hope to shape the consciousness of the young —a section which is open to new ideas and receptive to change. It won't do, for example, to merely project and glorify the achievements of the country, the benefits of which may not have reached our audience. Such an approach will soon lose credibility with the viewers and may even serve to increase the sense of alienation.

Instead we have to take up the more difficult and creative task of involving our audience in the problem of their own economic and social needs, of understanding the difficulties involved dispassionately, with a sense of optimism and self-confidence in their collective ability to solve these problems. It is important to build into the programming, as an integral approach, the concept that when people move to assert their rights they are also fulfilling the objectives of national policy. That this nation is their nation. Only with this positive and universal message will it be possible to nurture an active secularism, an attitude which rejects the facile explanations of communal and obscurantist ideologies, and resists the easy temptation to turn one's anger on one's neighbour instead of tackling the common enemy.

What will be the formats through which these messages could be portrayed ? Whether it be through dramatic serials, situation comedies, quiz programmes or through reportages, the source and inspiration must come from real life experiences. Learning by example can be a mode through which development successes can be generalised. Failure too can be used to avoid the repitition of mistakes and disillusionments. People's own words, their imagery and idiom must provide the guidelines to the professionals to develop their formats and contents.

What could be some of the themes for these programmes ? Literacy has to be a basic theme. Literacy which goes beyond alphabet skills into conceptual areas closely connected with people's lives. The literacy programmes could be based on the accumulated experiences and techniques developed by the agencies doing the best adult education work in the country.

Science is another such area. Programmes of great depth can be built around the problems of basic needs. Similarly, the natural environment of the views and their objects of everyday use can be the basis of programmes which are developed from the standpoint of the common underlying laws and principles. In this area significant work has been done by science popularisation organisations such as Kishore Bharati, Kerala Shastra Sahitya Parishad, Science Circle, and so on. Such work could provide the experimental basis for a new kind of science telecasting for our audience.

Health, both from the point of view of better health practices as well as from the standpoint of basic biology-microbes, living systems, and their interaction with an environment which is also a social system. Here too, the experience of health workers in both the public health system and voluntary organisations can be taken as the starting point.

Agriculture-not just better agricultural practices, but also the economic, biological and ecological systems which underly scientific agriculture.

History to develop a secular attitude, the lives of the common people in different places, during different historical and even pre-historical periods could be portrayed, bringing out their human qualities and circumstances, and freeing them from the popular myths which have created heroes and villains and prejudices about communities. Perhaps these periods could be seen through the eyes of children living in those times.

The fundamental approach to all the above themes would be—

*to take the everyday experience, culture and environment of the viewer, and treat it with respect, as a valuable source of knowledge.

*to develop an integrated and comprehensive approach, on the part of the viewer, to natural phenomena in their lives, as well as the social and historical processes of which they are a part.

*to show that reality is not compartmentalised, and therefore, neither can one's world view be compartmentalised.

* to encourage independent and critical analysis, making the method of science a habit of thinking. And a key to controlling both their natural and social environment.

The framework of ideas in this paper is presented in a fairly abstract manner. If these are acceptable to most of you, we must now use our combined experiences to concretise them. Beginning with tne methodology of generating programme briefs and formats to the criteria for the selection and training of production personnel, to the other more complex tasks like the working out of a cinematic language which is the vehicle for this new system of education. On the part of people like ourselves, such a task requires commitment, and the development of a culture of work which takes us forward from the lessons of SITE.

STRATEGY FOR MAKING VIDEO PROGRAMME PACKAGES ON HEALTH, NUTRITION AND FAMILY WELFARE FOR TRANSMISSION AS WELL AS NON-TRANSMISSION USE

V.N. Raina

TELEVISION holds tremendous potential as a means of educating and making the viewers conscientious about problems pertaining to their own health, in particular, and the environmental wholesomeness, in general. It is pertinent to recognise, however, that health and nutrition, important ingredients of life as they are, cannot be looked at in isolation from the Socio-cultural and economic aspects of the human populace, urban and rural, both. Dealing with health problems piecemeal, devoid of the interacting process of life, minimises the effectiveness of such programmes in generating a positive, rationalistic and scientific attitude towards solving these problems. Such a fragmentary approach becomes a dilutory effort leading to vague generalities, inconsequential in mobilising the viewers to desired action.

Before starting with the more concrete process of producing these programmes, it is important to arrive at a more in-depth analysis and understanding of the interlinkages in human affairs as well as the underlying causes at the root of diseases, both social and physiological in nature. Consequential upon a whole lot of factors, the changes (subtle and obvious) that have occurred in the social situation in as far as the life style, level of consciousness and value systems of the people are concerned, require to be studied to enable us to view and deal with these issues in a wider perspective. The technological developments, more specifically in the area of medicine and surgery, the effects and influences they have on the well-being or otherwise of the people, cannot be ignored. The potentials and limitations of the on-going medical systems, availability of and accessibility to the resources of care and good health for the average population, are other factors that need to be pondered over and taken into account. The ever-increasing gap between the growing infrastructural facility on the one side and constantly multiplying numbers that need them on the other, makes it imperative to arrive at alternatives that can help maintain a reasonable balance between the two.

Besides, the commercialization of medical system renders the proper use of such facilities beyond the means and reach of the larger chunk of our population. The culture of over-dependence on the modern and more sophisticated techniques of medical process have almost wiped out the localised systems of curing—even the most common and conventionally manageable ailments;—notwithstanding the hazards of potentially dangerous drugs when used more frequently and without proper medical guidance and supervision. In such a state of affairs identifying the local resources and means, educating the viewers regarding the advantages of preventive measures, emphasising the need for proper nutrition and planned family size, and demonstrating the possibilities of domestic cure, can lessen dependence on outside assistance and supplies, and go a long way in providing answers to the general health problems of the people who themselves happen to be the most valuable resource for their own health.

With this backdrop we may now proceed to work out a strategy for preparing video-programme packages—both for transmission as well as non-transmission use.

Scope and objectives

The general objectives of such a programme-package should be to :

(i) Sensitise the viewers towards the problems and needs pertaining to their health, nutrition, family size and their inter-relationship with the environmental realities—with a view to generate a more scientific and rationalistic attitude and approach in dealing with these problems (both immediate as well as long-term) and finding practically manageable solutions to tackle them effectively.

(ii) Stressing on self-help as one of the best ways to good health and helping the viewers to develop a sense of collectiveness and responsibility towards one another and encouraging them to be involved in the decisions about health.

The specific objectives would be as under :

(i) To apprise the viewers about the hazards of over-dependence and blind faith in any of the prevailing medical systems, emphasising the damage that indiscriminate use of drugs can do.

(ii) To sensitise the viewers about the environmental influences on their health, and the need for a clean and healthy environment.

(iii) To demonstrate the positive advantages of preventive measures as well as suggesting simple and effective means of coping with common, symptomatic ailments like diarrhoea, cold, indigestion etc.

(iv) Giving the viewers skills to promote good health and to treat minor illness and injuries by themselves.

(v) To make the viewers conscious about the maladies of mal-nutrition and unhygienic diet and suggest a more balanced diet system, possible within the average income-status.

(vi) To educate the audience about the possible ill-effects of some of the taboos and superstitions pertaining to pre-natal as well as post-natal problems among women and also the process of child-rearing (This shall be done in such a manner that their deep-rooted cultural feelings do not get hurt) and suggest scientific means of dealing with these issues.

N.B. : It may be emphasised that children and women shall form the core attention-group in as far as the priorities in the selection of diseases and problems as also some practically possible suggestions regarding health and well being, are concerned.

The pedagogical and communications approach

In order to attain the set objectives to the optimum possible level, we may adopt what can be termed as the integrated approach.

The integrated approach is the total approach, wherein the varied aspects of life that influence the human situation, are taken into account. "Too often health professionals and governments have tried to tell the people what was wrong, rather than encouraging the people to be involved in the decisions about health" (Lowell Levin—World Health).

On the media side, our experience shows that when it comes to making health programmes, it is generally the diseases, their symptoms, their causes and effects, possible remedies and preventive measures, that are taken up. Such single-slot disease centred approach does perhaps have its meaning, but it only scratches the surface. While the need for specific and detailed information cannot be overemphasised, by itself it does not suffice the cognitive requirements of the viewers in as far as their active involvement is concerned. The disease lies much deeper.

"There are social causes for much sickness and death, not just biological ones" (Lowell Levin). Focus on symptomatic aspects of diseases keep the human element in the background, reducing it to the secondary status, which in effect alienates the viewers from their problems. The viewer response to such programmes is only casual. While they gain in information, the will to take to new ideas, and apply the acquired knowledge in practice is not sufficiently stimulated. The gains as opposed to media efforts made as such are only peripheral. Not without reason though. The practical difficulties of treading on non-conventional paths are manifold and it becomes easier to stick to tested routes, however inadequate they might be.

While it becomes necessary to evoke the need for change, it is equally important to work out the modalities for such desired change within the framework of real situations as they exist, the preoccupations of the people that are being addressed, and practically of the suggestions put forward through these programmes. Some of the traditional values that are detrimental to development and change have to be cautiously and carefully questioned, taking the sensitivities of the viewers pertaining to their beliefs and customs into full cognizance. The approach should be such as can generate confidence among the viewers in as far as their personal security (physical as well as psychological) vis-a-vis the subject matter and presentation of these programmes is concerned.

Emphasising self-dependence and help, should form the main thrust in as far as the pedagogical aspects of these programmes are concerned.

As for the portrayal of characters and the events associated with them, the overall approach will have to be of positive attitude-building taking up both negative and positive elements that happen to be a part of the existent realities. The purpose is not showing things just as they are but also showing how they ought to be, or could be. The ultimate goal is not to frighten the viewers about the grimness of the situation, but letting them realise that grim and different though the situation is, it is possible to find ways of improving it to our benefit within the resources at our disposal as of now. One may call it an idealistic approach, but it is required as a part of the pedagogical process to make people more confident in themselves, in their own potentials. There is no Utopia, but there are pragmatic practical possibilities within the reach of human effort. The totality of the situation when taken care of in the process of designing, planning, executing and transmitting these programmes will go a long way in optimising positive viewer response and helping them to acquire the status of "praxis" the process of reflection and action—each leading to other.

As is evident, the integrated approach implies a wider canvas, a broader frame of reference. Our emphasis is on the people—their lives with its sweet and bitter experiences, their dreams and aspirations, their potentials and shortcomings, their varied day-to-day as well as long term problems. Blended with all these will be the problems of their health—their minor and major ailments, an analysis of the clinical and underlying causes of these diseases and the pros and cons of the current practices that they follow tackling these problems. All this will be coupled with suggestions regarding the possibilies of approaching these problems and seeking solutions in a scientific and rationalistic manner.

Social life in terms of events, interactions between people at different levels, concerns caused by historical as well as the ongoing influences and also the philosophic content of each individual life have a certain continuity, physical and abstract. It is, therefore, necessary that the spirit of these linkages and continuity gets reflected through these programmes.

FROM SITE TO INSAT

G.D. Shukul

THE DREAM of Dr. Vikram Sarabhai was realised when Satellite ATS-6 was used in 1975-76 to beam TV programmes to over 24,000 villages in the country spread over six States namely Andhra Pradesh, Bihar, Karnataka, A.P., Rajasthan and Orissa. SITE, even as an experiment, had a clear-cut objective—to utilize the year long communication link by extending TV coverage to the rural areas by way of specially designed programmes for education, social change and national integration.

SITE was an experiment while INSAT is the thing. The pace of expansion through INSAT-1B has been at a brisk pace. By the end of the 6th Plan (March-April 1985), 70 per cent of the population will be covered by television, which by then, will envelop the entire country in its magic. By 1985-86 there wlll be 20 production centres using 179 transmitters to carry the programmes to the audiences. A great achievement, but at the same time the responsibility at the programme end, gets enhanced manifold.

The latest working group set-up for "preparing software plan for Doordarshan, taking into consideration the main objective of assisting in the process of social and economic development of the country, is to act as an effective medium for providing information, education and entertainment brings out anomalies in the working of TV and impediments to be taken note of. The report by this Committee, headed by Prof. P.C. Joshi, apart from other things, gives perspective to the prevailing situation at the executive end of the ministry—Doordarshan.

It brings out the finer points which need attention for they come in the way of effective use of the medium. The report makes a special mention about the creative freedom for the professional communicator responsible for software and it clearly notes "day-to-day interference and encroachment in political and in administrative spheres in short caution against ending up into government planning of software - needs to be curbed." These have to be taken into cosnideration, if one is serious about the business of programming in any field. SITE was a big job which had been executed with a fair degree of success. Well, nobody denied this fact but we, or rather the people involved, could not get over it. We were totally awed by our success. Probably, the success was more than what we were capable of or expected of ourselves.

The SITE experiment was effective for positive gains as well as the negative points, indicated in the findings of assessors, where things went wrong or did not work in line with the expectations. It is another thing that what is generally heard and talked about is confined to positive gain alone. The shortfalls in the experiment are generally side tracked. Though, to my mind, the lapses which came to the fore, are more important than the achievements—because today in view of the INSAT system, we at least know the pitfalls and the ways to overcome them.

During SITE, hard pressed for time as it was, involved processes moved fast, and it seldom stood still for its portrait. Activity was at break-neck speed, agencies and individuals in the field were forging ahead as so much was at stake. Repetition of what went into SITE may not be possible in the late eighties ; what is more, there is a lot which needs reconsideration.

Take the software aspect of SITE. There was hardly time to experiment with modes in the preparation of the programme. As they say in Chinese, 'if you want to reach fast, keep to the old roads.' By and large, old routine and values in broadcasting, were followed. It is as much applicable in the areas of programmes for the special audiences i.e. women and children as any other. It may be difficult to come by evidence of breaking new ground in communicating with these special groups. Whatever success was achieved could perhaps be credited to the novelty of TV and not as much to experimenting with techniques in programmes suited to the requirements of audience in these categories.

Due to the time factor, the studies regarding the target audience were not very comprehensive and at times they overlooked or could not totally understand the related groups — that is by way of understanding the communities closely, appreciating their requirements consonant with learning processes different from what was within the experience of the producers catering to them. The groups were varied in their comprehension level and held divergent values in their life style. Although audience profiles were made available, in actual practice they failed to be of much help.

In a way even the basic needs for meaningful programming remained unfulfilled, which was rather unfortunate. Hence, there is every need to see now that the producers are well oriented to the clientele they are to serve. Incidentally, even in the earlier stages Dr. Sarabhai was aware of the necessity and had made provision for the production teams to tour the areas intensively. This aspect was somehow lost once the experiment materialized.

The other thing which went wrong was, sticking to the conventional lines set for programme-production inclusive of presentation. This contributed its bit to failures so far as communicating with the special audiences was concerned. It was duly reflected in the assessments. For example, in most of the rural areas women invariably do not view programmes along with the menfolk. This was known after months had passed and it was too late for any corrections.

The reference should equally be relevant where preparing programmes for children is concerned. Take for instance, 'drawing lessons' or items of 'cut (paper) flowers' which appeared to be a fantastic and interesting programme but practically considering the absence of the requisite materials to practice later, in the villages the programme naturally proved pointless. In this way, after a while the demarcation in the programmes for different sections of the audience was not clear and after a while it became free for all. I do not recall how much of it got recorded in the assessment reports but I do have some evidence of this bad (or lack of) planning which I had compiled during the period of SITE.

The programmes were planned and produced with the awareness that the selected groups were located in some of the most backward regions. No wonder the image of the potential audience was an ideal one and not what it actually was. How wrong the thinking was became apparent only when I undertook an intensive tour of these areas. This was after SITE was more than half way through. The first hand exposure with the audiences in their own environment did prove a revealing experience and quite outside of what I had expected.

Touring in the clusters, the viewing Centres, in three States—Rajasthan, Bihar and M.P. took me round 86 villages. Once I got to know the children and women, the erroneous picture I had held till then, began to fade. Instead of finding motley crowds of mentally dull and bored people, they (the children) were lively, vibrant specimens full of enthusiasm for the TV shows. They exhibited the eagerness to learn, react and could even decide as to what suited them most. As I said before, by the time the true picture registered, it was too late to make any radical changes in the programmes.

It may be well to record what I discovered, even though the means may not be acceptable to scientific assessors. The children by and large were found equipped with good comprehension. Their interest was not restricted to material falling into their share alone. They took equal interest in other programmes too. Most of them were able to reel out fixed points in the shows, acted as self-appointed publicity agents of TV shows, remembered salient points made in the utility programmes and conveyed the same to the adults and so on.

As regards women, one would say they were on the timid side, but only when I met them alone. In the reassuring presence of the opinion leaders in their respective communities, they opened up and discussed their requirements, aspirations, reacting to shows and pointing out where it had failed to reach them. This part is well covered in the scientifically carried out researches and hence there is no need to extend any further except for a few comments considered relevant.

There was general agreement about the need for instructional ideas going into the programmes and so also utility items including those on childcare, nutrition, suggestions for improved diet, occupations, counselling etc. This can have meaning by follow-up action of the points made, ideas given, at the receiving end not by itself but by a carefully organized activity introduced into the system, making it possible to fill gaps in comprehension by way of whatever additional information is required as help. By experience we already know that unless due care is taken, the message and idea going out to the audience is likely to get lost without a chance for putting into practice. Supportive literature in print is hardly the answer because of the high rate of illiteracy in the rural areas. The answer is in activised groups of viewers, at least in community viewing who can instil the need for putting the suggestions into practice.

Utilisation of programmes can be productive for the user if attention is given to audience involvement. It calls for educating the user by developing proper attitude to what goes out to him through the media. Their psychology, frame of mind has to be developed for better acceptance of the benefits offered through software. The involved processes in communicating with virgin minds of rural population through sophisticated means like INSAT somehow miss the point totally. Yet another lesson learnt during SITE certainly deserves better consideration now when INSAT has become a reality.

The point being made is in favour of maintaining a close touch with the audience by seeking their direct involvement. At this stage one may even go back to the experience of 'Teleclubs' formulated in 1959 when TV was first introduced in the country at Delhi. These were formed around groups of interested citizens with regular membership limited to twenty in each case to act as a nucleus in the local community of better informed persons having initiative. These activised groups viewed specially devised programmes on social education. The convenor of each Teleclub ensured post broadcast discussions, filling up gaps in comprehension where needed, deciding on follow-up action, seeking TV Centres help where necessary through regular weekly reports.

The teleclub idea was very successful and it was proved so by various assessments which includes one carried out by the UNESCO in 1962. At one time there were 170 active teleclubs functioning in and around Delhi both in the urban and rural areas. The success was possible by having a unit of staff with the responsibility of nursing the teleclub through close liaison with the members by post and personal visits. The teleclubs functioned well for a decade—that is, till due attention was paid to keep them alive and today the less talked about the subject the better.

It may be difficult to suggest the extent of any system's involvement in the use of its programmes; as regards initiative taken; kind of staff for the purpose of improving utilisation; training of users etc. It will presumably depend on the particular working conditions and prevailing circumstances at a given point of time. However, three general principles can be indicated for consideration.

(i) The system should take a closer and continuing interest in the use made for the system's output. It should encourage and help its users with training in the best use of what is offered.

(ii) The production staff should take direct interest in how their programmes are used. This data is collected by the Evaluation Teams. They should also take full interest in supportive literature on guides and materials. The feedback from the users in that case can be put to use in a constructive way for developing the programme output. It should also be used for midcourse changes in the production schedules wherever necessary.

(iii) Any opportunity for collaboration with the institutions/associations that represent the users of its materials should be warmly accepted. In fact the system should itself seek such a collaboration.

Avoiding to be a party to these broad principles can leave the producers sitting by themselves, unaware as to what their effort is really doing to their audiences. The most dramatic change in the matter of communication theory according to Wilbur Schramm is—"The gradual amendment of the idea of passive audience and replacement by the concept of highly selective audience, manipulating rather than being manipulated by a message—a full partner in the communication process"—appears applicable in the present context of communicating with special TV audiences in the INSAT situation. TV should remain an instrument of human relation, helping to live and work together, maintaining good health of the community.

For achieving this objective, to develop and sustain a poverty free living, the application of knowledge and skills at our disposal must be put to use.

The opportunities for acquiring knowledge and skills should be made available to the community. This will help individuals in making effective contribution towards a better life. Particular attention should be paid to rural areas where the bulk of the population lives and where the need for improvement is the greatest.

Women should be shown ways to devote their time in the best possible way for bringing up their children ; daughters given as much education as sons so that when the time comes they prove good mothers to their own children. No society has flourished without a degree of female emancipation. All womens' talks—family health, food, nutrition and home management needs should get supplemented through well devised programmes so that it is easy for women to adopt modern behaviour and attitude towards life which constantly keeps on changing with the times.

This is no place to get into details of the gaps and lapses noted during SITE, so that the going during INSAT-1B is smoother and more purposeful.

PROGRAMME PRODUCTION FOR CHILDREN

K. Vishwanath

BASED ON the experience of programme production for SITE (both science programmes for school children and Gujarati programmes for the Kheda audience) I have tried to pick out—almost at random—some learning experiences and issues which are fairly general, and which may be of interest for discussion. Each of the statements made below needs to be qualified with various "ifs", "buts", etc. and is not intended as a definite pronouncement. However, for the sake of brevity and to stimulate discussion, all qualifications have been dispensed with.

1. Science programmes as designed by us or for that matter, science as a subject does not do well for the age group of 5 to 12 years that we had in mind. This was also proved later by CTW New Year when they entered into the domain of science programme production and designed their science programme production for an upper age group 9 to 12. Apparently enough evidence has been found to establish that an attitude towards science is developed only at these ages.
2. We, wittingly or unwittingly, designed a definite method of madness in programme production which is especially applicable to instructional and non-formal educational areas. Broadly they are :

—Specifying the programme purpose
—Identifying the measurable objectives
—Identifying the target audience
—Determining issues fluency
—Re-examining purpose and objectives
—Specifying the information

—Determining the delivery channels
—Identifying and mobilizing intra-community and extra-community resources
—Organizing the delivery system
—Re-examining purpose, objectives and message(s)
—Creating and producing the sample message(s)
—Testing the sample message(s)
—Revising and reproducing the final message(s)
—Developing the training programme(s)
—Designing the evaluation component(s)
—Implementing the programme
—Preparing the report

Will it be necessary to follow the above pattern and if yes how to implement this methodology of programme production ?

3. Financial, technological and other considerations play more crucial roles in organizing software aspects. Why and how to overcome this so that software takes a precedence ?
4. Researchers, production personnel and content experts tend to make decisions which are more valid for the high income, urban based people who form a minority. How do you introduce participatory research so that the target audience is involved in programme production ?
5. Psychological and personal factors inhabit innovation, creativity and subject content. This point has been proved in many of the training camps we had conducted for science educators, University level teachers and production people. How do you overcome these factors when software is planned by specialised groups ?
6. Research inputs have higher acceptability when top bosses support it both administratively and creatively. How does one ensure that production people accept research findings with no hang-ups ?
7. In a multi-language country, dubbing is thrust upon creative personnel. Due to constant time considerations this enslaves them for life. In spite of various research

findings available, how does one persuade planners to desist from dubbing ?

8. Programmes with formats of plotted drama has higher appeal to children. Education through TV is a painful process. In the name of interest and entertainment, is it correct to go for sugar coated forms of presentation at the expense of educational content ?

9. It may be true to say that children have more grounding in the biological world of animals and plants than in the physical world of natural phenomena. Is it a true statement in the Indian context ?

10. A TV educational science programme does not have a life of its own, but is highly dependent upon intelligent pre-and post-telecast discussions by teachers who in turn need to be taken into confidence. What will be the other follow-ups for educational programmes for children ?

A VIDEO PRESENTATION FOR UNISPACE CONFERENCE : "TEACHER IN THE SKY"—"SCIENCE"

An All-India Educational Survey reveals that for every three children enrolled in primary school one eligible child is left out. And what happens to the three enrolled.

Two drop out before they complete 5 years in school and the one remaining goes on to complete about the 8th class.

A common reaction is to attribute the problem of population increases, but then that might be like putting the cart before the bullocks, for all we know.

Of all the explanations offered for the backwardness in the country's 4,70,000 primary schools, there is one problem that is so overwhelming that it is easier to overlook than to confront it. Where are the teachers to man these schools ?

In at least 3,000 schools, they say, there are no teachers at all.

In another 1,50,000 or over a third of the country's schools, the total staff strength in each is—one.

The activities of teaching and learning under such conditions have a powerful tendency to be oriented to rote memorization.

If "mugging-up" can be purposeless in nursery rhymes, how

much more so must it be in the sciences ?

Science still exists for many of us in another world, in text books and labs. No wonder then that our teaching of science seldom produces meaning in our daily lives or a scientific temper.

In the Satellite Instructional Television Experiment, SITE for short, we were working outside the treadmill of a school syllabus. We had to reach large numbers of village children from 6 to 13 years. We were also dealing with teachers with rather modest accomplishments, many of them high school drop-outs themselves.

While these might easily have been crippling conditions for a science teaching exercise, it was in reality a boon. It was an excellent opportunity to show science as a way of understanding common place phenomena. Science could be experienced directly, not as the exotic activity of a priveleged elite but as an attitude to the world around us, to be shared by the rich and the poor, with or without an expensive layout or sophisticated apparatus. The staff enunciated a philosophy, a credo, to guide their work in the science programmes. The producers called it a new gospel, a mantra.

Doing science in the immediate environment also dissolved the restrictive distinctions across physics, chemistry, biology, and so on and the isolation of topics within them. It was, for all of us, a rediscovery of science through an ecological perspective.

Some excerpts from the programmes. Here are good and bad bacteria in dialogue about their lives and deeds.

In another programme a snake appears as an enemy of man, but a donkey reveals the friend in him.

But television can be as authoritarian as an orthodox lab. Here is a character leaving the confines of a TV set to interact with his audience. So did many of the programme staff learn with their rural audience and learn from them.

What did we learn from SITE about science teaching ?

We must confess that exposure for 22 minutes twice a week in one year was perhaps too little to produce any dramatic change.

An evaluation study indicated that while the attitude of seeking information from sources other than conventional class-rooms did show gains, there was no significant change in scholastic achievement.

The fact that the drop-out rate or school attendance was not affected by the introduction of TV, seemed to confirm that factors other than attraction for education were at play.

One perceptive comment made at the end of SITE, not by a teacher or social scientist, but by a small boy from an interior village was . . . . . .

"The relief that the TV programme provided from classroom drudgery is lost, and we will be miserable and lonely as before."

SITE conducted special programmes for teachers too. 50,000 teachers were the target audience for enriched refreshers in science and mathematics. The success of the programmes and its need was recognised more fully only after the project, and we wished it could have been a continuous and committed affair between the teacher and the medium.

According to the estimate made earlier, if more than 1.7 million teachers need to be re-oriented and trained, the problem appears really to be one of vast coverage in minimum time. The choice of a technology medium mix is therefore crucial to the task. Satellite Television, we believe, can be of help.

Years after the programme, our reflection continues :

> What needs of learning are served by our methods of teaching ?
>
> Or these methods of learning perhaps our needs of teaching ?

A letter from an interested observer seemed to echo our own thoughts on the experience. He said :

> "this is an exercise in planting trees not in delivering timber. Sure, timber is nice to have. Don't leave them all out, but be very sure to nurture seedlings, to admire new growth and to foster it."

Epilogue

The effort continues. With the Indian national satellite in orbit, India moves from conception to realisation, from experiment to operation, from SITE to INSAT. Designed as the linchpin of the country's communication network, INSAT will service telecommunication, television broadcasts, and meteorology. This space venture would very shortly make the chicken mesh antenna a permanent feature on the terraces and grounds of thousands of village schools in India.

TELEVISION FOR WOMEN EXPERIENCES FROM SITE AND POST-SITE

Neeraja Vohra and *S.V.S. Chowdhary*

THE PRESTIGIOUS Satellite Instructional Television Experiment (SITE) from August 1, 1975 to July 31, 1976, was among the most advanced and largest experiment on human communication. During this experiment TV could be made accessible to the residents of 2,340 remote villages of six states having four linguistic groups.

The experiences of SITE showed that TV has been accepted by the villagers. Except agriculture, the significant gain was observed in all developmental areas such as health, hygiene, children, women, animal husbandry, political socialization and overall modernity among the illiterates.

The rich experiences of SITE motivated the policy makers/ media planners to continue the instructional programmes through terrestrial transmitters in all the six states. The experiment was made a continuous process of production, research and utilization.

SITE was an experiment with clear cut objectives of studying the existing rural communication process, role of TV as a new medium and the process of change brought about by TV in the rural area at micro-level. The total human and financial resources were mobilized to make SITE a success.

The enthusiasm and motivation was lost in the business of mass production with meagre facilities of man power and machinery. The concept of rural programmes has been gradually diluted due to the presence of educated, influential and vocal urban elites. The programmes produced by SITE centres could have neither rural nor urban orientation.

Programme for women

In view of the specific problems of women folk, besides the general adult programmes, there were special programmes for women during SITE. Several researches conducted during SITE have revealed that there was significant impact of TV programmes on women. During post SITE period, there is a separate chunk in the transmission schedule of all the Upgrah Doordarshan Kendras. Before taking up the quality and content of womens programmes, it is essential to have a look at the receiving end.

The long experiences and research studies have revealed that almost negligible number of females come to view the programmes on Community television. Some ladies from nearby houses however, have been observed viewing the feature films on television. It can almost be generalised that majority of women do not view TV programmes in the rural area. The important reasons for not viewing TV programmes are :

(i) The women of high socio-economic group and young girls are discouraged to come to public places like chaupal or school to attend such gatherings,

(ii) The female folks of lower socio-economic status hardly find spare time in the evening to view TV programmes. After coming from the fields or work they are engaged in domestic work. It is, therefore, doubtful that they can give time to view our so-called developmental women's programmes,

(iii) The language of the programme is Hindi which is difficult for the rural women to follow particularly the illiterate and semi-literates. The speed of delivery of the participants is generally fast and the message many a times, goes over the heads of rural folk,

(iv) Even the developmental programmes failed to attract the rural women. The programmes are not need-oriented to suit their environment and economic status. The inputs given through these programmes are not supported by the development/user agencies. Therefore, many times the programme messages create frustration among the viewers as no infrastructure is available to utilize it,

(v) In villages the TV sets are installed in the primary school building which is generally far off from the residential area. Neither village elders nor the women themselves like to go out of the home during the night to view TV programmes. The parents-husbands do not allow their young daughters/wives to watch the TV programme along with fellow villagers.

Regarding the quality of programmes, critics, psychologists, sociologists, educators, and social reformers are of the opinion that women programmes are of poor quality in content and presentation. It is agreed that our programmes could not motivate the rural women to come out of misapprehensions, social evils etc. Yet, not a single script/material has been received so far suggesting creative media strategy. The programmes, however, are always produced on scripts prepared by eminent experts.

Suggested model for INSAT

After SITE, INSAT is now in operation to provide signals to 70 per cent of the total population in India. To make optimum use of INSAT Television signals, it is important to produce effective programmes and ensure its utilization by the target audience/the consumers. The following points are being put to the august body for intensive consideration.

(i) Electricity should be made available during transmission hours.

(ii) Proper maintenance of TV sets should be ensured.

(iii) There should be effective provision to ensure regular operation of TV sets in school as well as evening hours. There should be separate community TV centres for women. To start with a set can be provided to each ANM centre or any other suitable place.

(iv) The TV messages should be supported and followed by inter-personal communication of developmental agencies. The necessary infrastructure should be made available so that the message can be utilized.

(v) The creative thinkers-communicators, psychologists,

educators should be motivated to come forward to contribute substantially in producing effective and relevant programmes for the target group, particularly children and women.

(vi) The programme makers should be well aware of the needs and characteristics of the target audience. Proper research input should be made available at each stage of production.

(vii) Quick and effective feedback should be made available.

(viii) The necessary facilities should be provided to the programme makers.

(ix) There should be sufficient flexibility to produce creative media product as it requires a lot of effort, planning, time and facilities.

(x) Outdoor shooting should be encouraged.

MANAGEMENT AND UTILISATION

EXPERIENCES OF RADIO WORKSHOP ON MATERNAL AND CHILD CARE IN THE SOUTHERN STATES

T.P. Balagopalan

I WISH TO highlight through this paper the methodology adopted in the conduct of three Radio workshops in the States of Kerala, Tamil Nadu and Karnataka on "Maternal and Child Care" and the subsequent follow up measures taken.

The methodology though varied from state to state, to some extent, the core remained the same.

The duration of the workshops in all the cases was five days. The participants were from all the Radio Stations and Doordarshan of the concerned States, as well as officials from village to State levels from departments like Health, Rural Development, Social Welfare, Adult and Non formal education who are responsible for the implementation of the programmes of maternal and child care. In addition, representatives of village level mahila mandals (tribals and harijans) from the rural areas and slum dwellers from urban areas had also participated.

The Health Department was represented by the Auxiliary Nurse Midwifes, block health extension workers, medical officers of Primary Health Centres in the jurisdiction of the different Radio Stations, DHOs, Assistant Directors of Health, as well as professors in gynaecology, paediatrics of the Medical Colleges. The Social Welfare Department was represented by Balasevikas, anganwadi workers, supervisors, CDPOs, District Social Welfare Officer, Assistant Director of Social Welfare Gramasevikas, Mukhya Sevikas, BDOs, District Women Welfare Officers, Assistant Development Commissioners etc., represented the Rural Development

Department. All India Radio stations were represented by the Station Directors, and producers of the various programmes. The Non-formal and Adult Education Department was represented by animators at the village, Project Officer for Non-formal Education at District and Assistant Director at the State levels.

We have taken a cross section of the beneficiaries, especially from the poor section and also the officers of the various departments connected with the programme from the village to the State levels from various parts of the State duly taking into account the locations of radio stations with the intention of getting the real problems as well as the conventions, faith, beliefs and maladies that are prevailing in the various parts of a State and suggest remedial measures.

At the outset, all the specialists as well as officials from village to the State levels and non-official village level women representatives sat together and identified the various problems that are being faced by the rural as well as urban poor in respect of maternal and child care, particularly in respect of the pregnant women and children upto the age of five. Each participant was made to identify a few problems and explain them in the combined session. It was really a very educative process even for the organisers to find the rural, tribal as well as the slum women coming forward with their problems as well as the various conventions and beliefs which are prevalent in various parts of a State. All the problems identified were subsequently tabulated, duly deleting repetitions, and a final picture was drawn up in respect of the maladies of the children from minus nine months to five years and also the various issues which are relevant in respect of the care of pregnant women and children.

After sorting out the maladies and connected issues as mentioned above, the participants of the workshop were divided into five groups and the materials prepared were assigned to each group for further discussion on each and every item, and to identify about two dozen messages that could be presented through broadcasts from AIR.

Each group had specialists in gynaecology, paediatrics (professors of the Medical Colleges), Medical Officer of HPC,

ANM, DHO, Assistant Director Health Services, Grama Sevika, Mukhya Sevika, supervisor (ICDS), Block Development Officer, CDPO, District Social Welfare Officer, Assistant Director of Social Welfare Office, Assistant Development Commissioner, animator/balasevika/anganwadi worker, representatives of mahila mandal, etc. The group functioned as one team as all were members of the group. This helped in getting more and more information from the field workers and the job of specialists was confined mostly to suggesting solutions for their acceptance. The interaction between ANM to Assistant Director of Health and Professors of Medical Colleges and Station Directors and Producers of All India Radio, Grama Sevika and anganwadi worker to the Assistant Directors of various departments, mahila mandal workers (including harijans and tribal women) upto the specialists was exciting and it created a feeling of equal participation.

After getting the messages identified by each group, they met again in a plenary session and discussed the various measures suggested by all the groups and the common messages thus identified were finally selected. In selecting the messages, the experiences of the producers and station directors were also taken into account so that they could project the messages in an appropriate format for the broadcast.

After the final selection of the messages, these were divided into five parts and each part was given to the group for presentation of synopsis under each message. On the finalisation of the synopsis, the plenary session was held again and the synopsis in respect of each message was thrashed out. The plenary then nominated a group of specialists from the Health, AIR, Social Welfare and Rural Development and entrusted them with the responsibility of finalising the write-up in respect of each message which could be ultimately used by the radio stations as a base for bro adcast.

One important decision taken was that the radio stations should have the freedom to choose the format for each message that could be broadcasted.

Selected messages were translated into certain formats by the radio stations and the broadcast matter was prepared.

This broadcast matter recorded in different formats in cassettes by the radio stations was taken to the villages and field-tested with the help of rural women assembled in groups for listening. This exercise was done by each group in different villages with different messages and the feedback was brought to the plenary session and they had a very interesting and useful discussion. This helped the producers as well as the Station Directors of AIR to a very great extent to understand how the programmes are being received by the listener beneficiaries.

Regarding the timing of the broadcasts, there was no unanimous view. As such we had a consensus on the timing for each radio station area and left the matter to the discretion of the radio stations.

As far as Tamil Nadu was concerned, we printed a booklet containing all the messages with detailed write-up in respect of each message in Tamil and supplied to the AIR stations in the State, including Pondicherry. The write-up in respect of Kerala State has been finalised by the specialists and it is being printed with pictorial illustrations. As far as the Karnataka State is concerned, the write-up is being finalised.

The importance, usefulness and the necessity of group listening for issues on maternal and child care were discussed. There was a difference of opinion among the participants that availability of radios in almost all homes will affect group listening. It was decided that people have to be educated and convinced about the necessity of group listening, interaction, discussion and processing of questions for the radio stations on each broadcast.

After the conclusion of the workshop, listeners were organised in Tamil Nadu and conveners, chairpersons, field functionaries etc. were given training in group listening, discussion on the messages and preparation of questions for the radio stations for getting additional information etc.

The special series of broadcasts started in Tamil Nadu on the messages are just over and we have taken up a study to evaluate the impact of the messages on the members of the listener groups—how far they have understood and benefited and are adopting the format as well as the content of the messages and how they were received by the listeners etc. The evaluation report which is being prepared by the Extension Directorate of the Tamil Nadu Agricultural University is expected to be ready by the end of this month.

Duly taking into account our experiences in broadcasting messages through the AIR Stations in Tamil Nadu, we held discussions with the officials connected with the Doordarshan, Madras, who have also participated in our earlier workshop for finding out how best Doordarshan could also be used for propagating the messages. We have now taken a decision to accept the very same messages already identified and televise them in the appropriate formats through the Madras Doordarshan most probably from January 1985 onwards.

One advantage with Doordarshan programme, we feel, is that group listening among the poor people is a must and could be made possible as all cannot afford to have television sets. However, the most important aspect to be taken into consideration is the timing of such telecasts. The messages should be given in understandable and interesting formats through Doordarshan at a time suitable to the poor women in rural-slum areas. We are now organising television groups like radio listeners groups in the city and suburban areas of Madras.

The disadvantage for this zone is that even though we have a good number of Doordarshan low power transmitters telecasting the national programmes, there are no independent TV stations except Madras. There is also no arrangement for relay from Madras to the other Stations in the State. As far as Bangalore and Trivandrum are concerned, they wiil start their own independent programmes for a few hours shortly. All other stations are only telecasting the national programmes. In view of this, the Doordarshan programme which we intend to telecast will benefit only people in Madras city and suburban areas in Chingleput and North Arcot Districts.

TV, WOMEN AND CHILDREN
Some Thoughts

B.S. Bhatia

TV, WOMEN and children have a special relationship. Whenever and wherever a TV set is on, children form a substantial and dedicated part of the audience. Even in a community viewing situation, both SITE and Kheda experiences have indicated that more than 50 per cent of the audience consists of children. They are in the formative years of their life and are avid viewers who can easily carry the impressions that the medium creates on their minds. Women have shown a great potential to learn from TV. The SITE results indicate that it was the illiterate women that gained the most from TV. Thus, both qualitatively and quantitatively, women and children have a special relationship to TV and therefore they deserve special attention.

But when we talk of women and children in general, we are talking of a very large audience. In fact the term women and children would cover about 70 per cent of the population of India. It is, therefore, necessary to segment this audience into finer categories to enable effective use of the media. I do not intend to go into a systematic audience segmentation exercise here but only try to indicate some important categories and issues related to programming for them.

Planning TV for children

All child psychologists agree that children pass through a number of stages from a learning point of view. Television inputs for each category have to be different. The first category when the child is still not a TV viewer, is that of infants. Infants are not TV viewers but their problems need special attention. In India today the infant mortality rate is quite high.

In fact, it is higher than some neighbouring countries like Sri Lanka. It is also an important factor which affects the birth rate in the country. It is, therefore, a problem which needs attention. The programmes and problems of infants would of course be aimed at parents, and could cover areas like immunisation, breast-feeding, and care during common infant problems like diarrhoea.

Next category would be the pre-school or the early school child. Almost no effort has been made for TV programming for this category in India. One has heard a great deal about American efforts like Sesame Street, etc. for this category. It is, of course, well known that with the use of puppets, and animation etc., this category of audience can be converted into dedicated viewers. But a great deal of planned effort is required for which we are not at all equipped.

The school going child beyond the age of 8 or so can pay greater attention to TV and learn more systematically. Attempts were made during SITE to make science programmes for the category 6 to 12. But it was found that the programmes were more suitable for the higher age group of 9 to 12 years. Subsequently we made attempts for student of Std. V and VI (age 10 to 12). The attempts was to convert textbook lesson's of Gujarati, Science and Social Studies subjects into TV programmes. It was found that these programmes were very keenly watched and easily comprehended. Here again the use of puppets made even dry subjects very interesting. It is also learnt from earlier efforts of producing serials like "*Nandu Indu*" and "Vad thi mota Teta" for children that use of fantasy is an important element in children's programming and can be used for triggering their imagination, but planned children's programming needs much greater effort than most Indian organisations are prepared to invest. The lack of effort leads to drab programmes and the medium is unnecessarily blamed.

Planning TV for women

In the Indian society the basic issue to be dealt with is the value of a girl child. Traditionally the birth of a girl child is not necessarily considered to be a happy occasion. This problem has to be tackled and again this category of programmes has to be aimed at the parents. Closely linked with this issue is the treatment of the girl child during the early years. This includes her education and the role for which she is trained in the formative years. Traditionally, in the Indian society the education of the girl is neglected and the role she is trained for is that of a house-wife. Following this stage are the problems related to marriage including the age of marriage, the process of selection of a match, the dowry system etc. Linked with the perception of the value of a girl child is also the problem and the recognition of the contribution of women. The domestic work looked after by women does not get any recognition. It is also noticed that the value of women is directly linked to her economic independence. It is therefore necessary to train women for some kind of economic activity to develop economic independence.

We have made two serious attempts at programming for women. A serial called "*Jagine Joun To*" aimed at comparing the treatment of a girl child with that of a body at various stages in growth. It compares the celebrations at the time of birth, the difference in education etc. The second serial *Nari-Tu-Narayani* was an attempt at motivating women to organise themselves into co-operatives to take up economically viable activities.

Men as a target audience

While the TV programmes should aim at women and children, it is also essential that men are sensitised to the problems of women and children. In the society as it is today, men dominate decision making and unless men understand these issues, change for the betterment of women and children will only meet with greater resistance. It is essential that men are also addressed on TV and are sensitised to these problems specially to the problems of women.

Systems issues

While women and children form a special audience they also have special problems. The most important problem is that of access to the media. Women, specially in the rural areas, have little or no access to the media. Even in villages where community sets are available, the women would first of all have no time to come and watch TV. They are busy working in the field all during the day and have to work at home in the evenings. It is therefore very difficult to bring this audience to the TV set. However, it is found that if a specific day and time is ear-marked for women and if programmes are clearly of their interest, they make it a point to come at least on that day. And even if they can, they would be forced to sit far away from the crowd in a corner and they would find it difficult to view TV in a community viewing situation. It is essential that some thought is given to creating special viewing situations for them. This could be in *mahila mandals* or such women organisations.

For the production of children and women's programmes specialised personnel and skills are required. Unfortunately, in India we do not have specially identified people working only for children's programming or women's programming. It is essential that we create such specialised teams. It is also essential that these teams develop a certain commitment to the task that they have on hand. It is essential to raise a cadre of producers, trained and committed to women's and children's programming.

Utilisation

Utilisation, especially in a broadcast mode, is a very difficult proposition. Expecting the user agencies to conduct follow up activities simultaneously in the field has a host of coordination and logistic problems. This cannot be done on a routine basis.

One possibility of effective utilisation is to conduct it in a "Campaign" mode. In this mode TV and other broadcasting media can play a very important information dissemination and support role. The user agencies should discuss with the media, well in advance, their campaign details, and the support requirements. The total content and schedule for the campaign should be provided by the user agencies and the support monitored.

Another situation in which proper utilisation can be expected is the use of TV in a "Non-broadcast" mode. With the costs of TV and VCR's decreasing and their portability increasing, the use of video as an extension tool does hold out some promise. This can enable closed door viewing with selected target groups and intense intimate discussions and other follow-up like demonstration, distribution of material etc. The recent expansion of TV in the country is making production of video programmes easier day-by-day. The user agencies should be able to get good material produced from a variety of sources and use it in a non-broadcast mode.

Overall Credo

While the above efforts are no doubt required to generate appropriate and effective programmes for women and children, a more fundamental requirement is that of a "Credo" for the broadcasting organisation. While the general objectives of broadcasting may be to educate, inform and entertain, it is very essential to define what should not be done. This is even more important when we talk of women and children as our target audience.

It is very essential that the broadcasting organisation defines for itself a framework which says that programmes reinforcing superstitions, or programmes reinforcing the traditional negative image of women will not be shown at all on TV. It is counter productive to show films wherein the women accepting all oppression of the husband, family and society is glorified. The effect of one such programme reinforcing traditional negative values is to wipe out the effects of the new positive values one is trying to incorporate. Even if the telecast of such negative programmes is stopped, it would be a significant achievement.

PROGRAMME PRODUCTION FOR CHILDREN—Some Management Issues

Kiran Karnik

DURING SITE, a large proportion of the children's programmes were produced in ISRO's Bombay SITE studio, which was a facility dedicated fully to this purpose only. Its function was, in fact, defined even more specifically : the production of science education programmes for children. It is desirable/necessary to have such dedicated production facilities for children's programmes.

Similarly, the producers in this studio too were working only on children's programmes. On the other hand, at ISRO's Ahmedabad studio – then and now – producers make a variety of programmes and no producer is dedicated specially or only to children's programmes. Is it necessary to have dedicated producers who specialise in programmes for children ?

In most cases, producers of children's programmes are professionals in production. Only in the case of formal school education has ISRO used teachers (with only brief training in production) to make programmes. On the other hand, the SITEs propose to use educators – after due training – for programme production. In a different field, ISRO had trained veterinarians from Amul to produce the animal husbandry programmes. Is it then better to use a "child expert" (teacher, child psychologist, etc.) rather than a "production expert" as Producer ?

Creativity has been recognised as a key element for successful programming. This requires not only individual creativity, but an atmosphere, mechanisms and structuring within the organisation to foster and promote this. Is such "organisational creativity" feasible within the producers and structures of government organisations or does one necessarily have to think of an independent/autonomous structure for this aspect ?

As obvious aspect of children's programming is production in the "team-mode" involving, amongst others, a content-expert, child psychologist and a communications researcher, besides the production personnel. These persons must form a cohesive team and must be an integral part of the system. What structures and mechanisms are required to ensure that the team is an organic whole : a fusion of different expertise rather than a mere mixture ?

During SITE, enrichment programmes for 5-12 years old children were produced. Subsequently, we have experience in Kheda of producing both formal school education and enrichment programmes. Many entertainment programmes too have been produced, with a subtle "educational" content and also a very carefully planned, painstakingly made series to promote innovation. Whereas the SITE enrichment programmes were viewed in the controlled situation of a school classroom during school hours, the Kheda school-education programmes are transmitted in the evening and viewed by children along with adults in the general viewing situation. Should the children's programmes be shown in-school as in SITE ? Should they focus tightly on the school syllabus or be of a general/enrichment type ? Which age-group is the priority audience ?

During SITE, considerable effort went into generating, translating and distributing printed material to the school-teachers, as a part of the utilisation effort. A wall-paper for children was also prepared, translated, printed and distributed. What is the extent of utilisation support that must be a part of the communication strategy and how can this be done ? Which agency should undertake responsibility of preparing and distributing this material ?

Most of the effort in this field has so far concentrated on the 5+ age-group. Is there need to shift the focus or at least some proportion of the programmes towards pre-school children ?

INSAT EXPERIENCES
Candid Scenes from Andhra Pradesh

B.S.S. Rao and *B.V. Sharma*

TINY TRANSMITTER BOOM

A CRASH programme with an outlay of Rs. 68 crores was announced by Ministry of Information and Broadcasting in July last year for rapid expansion of television facility in the country. Under this special plan almost one TV transmitter a day has been the installation rate during the past few months. With a total strength of 180 transmitters—most of them linked to Delhi via INSAT—it is assured that by the year end Doordarshan's coverage would be extended to 70 per cent of the population.

As one of the six selected clusters, Andhra Pradesh has had the privilege of receiving TV programmes during the 1975-76 Satellite Instructional Television Experiment (SITE). Subsequently under the SITE continuity scheme, a high power transmitter (HPT-100 kw) was installed at Hyderabad in October 1977. Asiad brought the tiny low power transmitter (LPT-100 Watt) to Kakinada in November 1982.

Under the TV expansion scheme, drawn up for execution during the Sixth Five Year Plan (1980-85), it was originally proposed to have one high power transmitter (10 kw) at Vijayawada connected to Hyderabad. However, after the announcement of the crash programme, the plan was altered to have as many as 13 transmitters in the State by March 1985. Thus, these came in quick succession, the 1 kw transmitter at Vijayawada and 12 tiny transmitters (100 Watt) at Tirupati, Nellore, Cuddapah, Karimnagar, Visakhapatnam, Nizamabad, Warangal, Rajahmundry, Kurnool, Adoni, Anantapur and Mahabubnagar (Map-1).

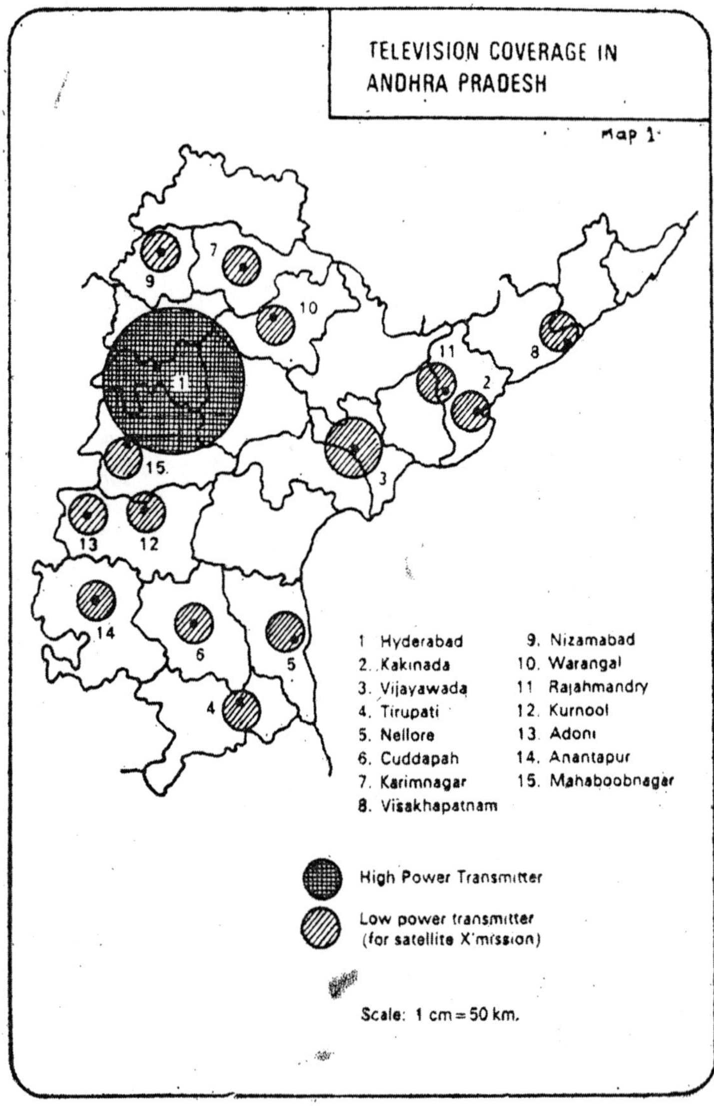
TELEVISION COVERAGE IN ANDHRA PRADESH
Map 1
1. Hyderabad
2. Kakinada
3. Vijayawada
4. Tirupati
5. Nellore
6. Cuddapah
7. Karimnagar
8. Visakhapatnam
9. Nizamabad
10. Warangal
11. Rajahmandry
12. Kurnool
13. Adoni
14. Anantapur
15. Mahaboobnagar
High Power Transmitter
Low power transmitter (for satellite X'mission)
Scale: 1 cm = 50 km.

The State has since got the full complement of its sanctioned strength and no more TV centres are expected to be set up in the near future. However, the present low power transmitters at Vijayawada and Visakhapatnam are likely to be replaced with high power transmitters after some time.

Seventy per cent population coverage—a myth

The present situation is a far cry from the goal of bringing 70 per cent of the State's five and a half crore population within the reach of television. Even with liberal estimates, not more than 80-90 lakhs people (17%) would be in a position to tap TV signals radiated either from Hyderabad or from Delhi via INSAT (Map-2).*

When we look beyond the physical possibilities, the actual picture is more distressing. Thc State has about 875 community sets to serve a population of about 18-20 lakhs in rural areas. The number of domestic sets in towns and peripheries is assumed to be around 2.5 lakhs** and these would not be accessible to more than 2 -30 lakhs persons. Thus, even on the higher side, there would hardly be 45-50 lakhs persons having exposure to TV. This restricts the potential reach of TV to about 10% of the State's population even in ideal conditions like total interface with all available sets.

Loose ends in community viewing

One of the critical factors in rural TV communication is the operation of an effective delivery system. During SITE, despite the best managerial capabilities and technical skills, ISRO was unable to eliminate the losses in exposure due to seepage in delivery. Problems like indifference of the custodians, mishandling of the sets, operational difficulties in set maintenance, etc. were frequently encountered.

Doordarshan, which handled the management of the community TV scheme at the post SITE centres, faced a host of problems due to shortage of manpower, transport bottlenecks

*While Hyderabad covers about 35 lakhs population, the 14 LPTs may be covering around 50 lakhs persons.

**Precise figures are not available.

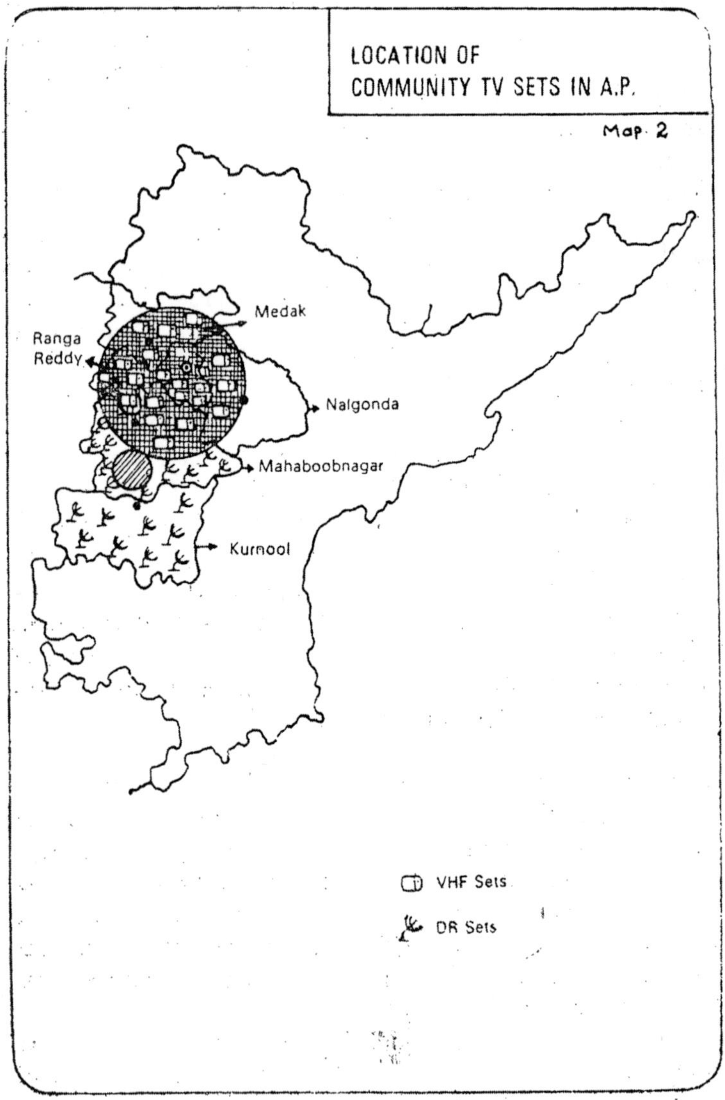
LOCATION OF
COMMUNITY TV SETS IN A.P.
Map 2
Medak
Ranga
Reddy
Nalgonda
Mahaboobnagar
Kurnool
VHF Sets
DR Sets

and inadequate support from the local administration.

Under the INSAT utilisation plan, the Central Government transferred the entire responsibility of the execution of the community TV scheme to the State Governments. In Andhra Pradesh the Commissionerate of Information & Public Relations is in overall charge of the administration of the scheme. Its Radio Engineering Division looks after the installation and maintenance of the conventional VHF sets in the coverage area of Hyderabad ground transmitter. Outside this zone, where the Direct Reception Sets (DRS) are planned for reception through INSAT, the scheme is entrusted to the Electronic Corporation of India (ECIL).

DRS in bad shape

Under the DRS scheme the augmented TV receiver sets were installed in 375 villages. Their distribution is indicated below :

District	*No. of sets*
Mahabubnagar	201
Kurnool	174
Total	375

Most of the DRS sets are said to be located in school buildings to facilitate group viewing among primary school children as well as adults.

Recently the Audience Research Unit of the Hyderabad TV Centre conducted 100 per cent physical verification of the sets in three talukas of Mahabubnagar district and three talukas of Kurnool district. The verification exercise covering about 75 villages seems to have revealed that 60-70 per cent of the sets were not functioning. The main reason attributed to this unhappy situation is that ECIL was only responsible for the commissioning of the sets and not for their maintenance. Though occasionally its field staff attend to minor complaints, the organisation has not been entrusted with the responsibility of periodical maintenance. Taking into consideration the very high incidence of breakdowns and other irregularities in set operation, the Centre is thinking of evolving a system for obtaining feedback on set operation.

Significant rate of breakdowns in VHF sets too

Reports are equally disturbing in respect of the functioning of the normal VHF community TV sets. Hyderabad zone has 502 sets and their position as gathered from the Radio Engineer's Office (Information deptt.) is given below :

TABLE 1 : **Position of VHF community TV sets in Hyderabad zone (as on 1-10-84)**

District	Sets located in gram panchayats		Sets located in schools		Total	
	No.	% not working	No.	% not working	No.	% not working
Ranga Reddy	124	16.9	78	23.0	202	19.3
Mahabubnagar	74	40.5	29	27.6	103	36.8
Medak	76	38.1	29	27.6	105	35.2
Nalgonda	68	8.2	24	16.6	92	10.9
Total	342	25.1	160	23.7	502	24.7

With as many as 25 per cent of the sets going out of order at frequent intervals, the maintenance units are not able to attend promptly to the complaint calls. The Ranga Reddy District Deputy Engineer's office which has 202 sets in its jurisdiction has only two technicians. It receives 10-15 complaints a month. Under the circumstances, an average time lag of 15 days is reported between the receipt of the complaint and the repair of the set.

Delhi umbrella

The 14 Low Power Transmitters hang on to Delhi for transmission of programmes via INSAT. Except for the irrelevant 40 mts. of area-specific rural programmes designed for Hyderabad cluster, the audience seldom receives programmes in Telugu language. The frustrating experience of watching Hindi programmes (which most of the people do not comprehend in the coverage area of the LPTs) is pictorially presented in Fig. 1. The picture depicts the pain and pleasure of TV watching in an upper-middle class family at Rajahmundry. The Hindi scare compels many TV owners to keep their sets closed,

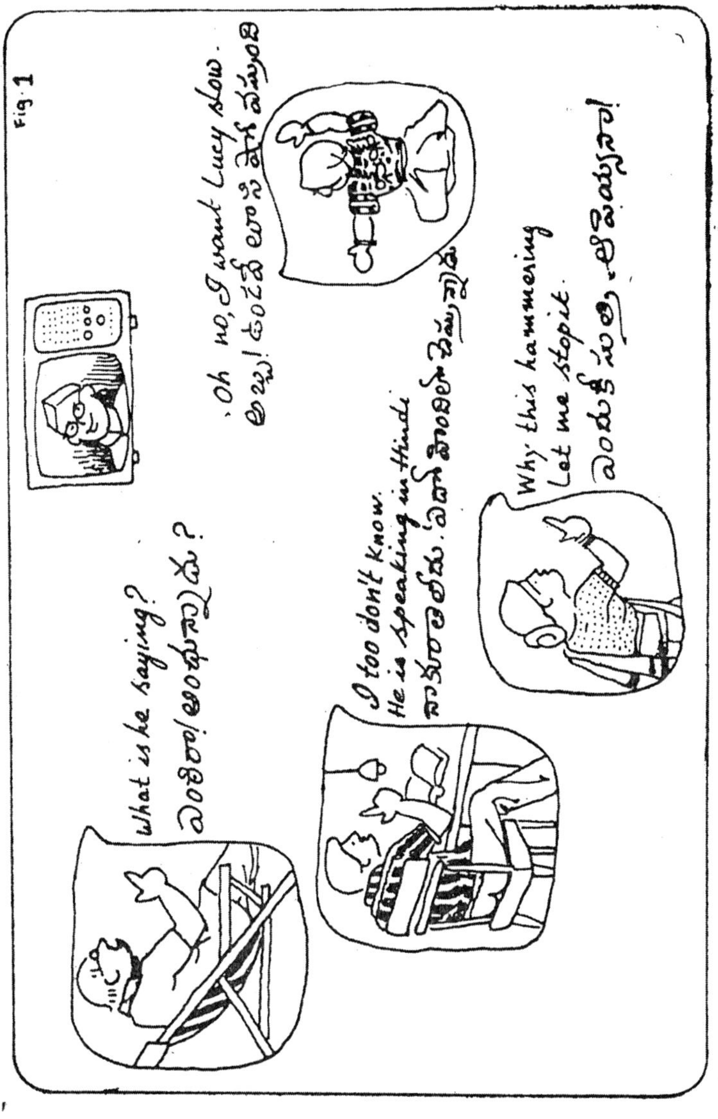
What is he saying?
I too don't know.
He is speaking in Hindi
Why this hammering
Let me stopit.
Oh no, I want Lucy show.

Fig. 1

save for the film-based entertainment items.

Two faces of Hyderabad TV

As an Upagraha Doordarshan Kendra, Hyderabad is expected to transmit essentially developmental programmes. However, because of the concentration of domestic viewing in Hyderabad city and suburbs, the service turns out to be largely entertainment-oriented. For illustration, the telecasts of the Centre (other than ETV) were analysed for a week (7-13 October 1984). The programmes, lasting for nearly 42 hours of transmission, reflected a composition presented in Table 2.

TABLE 2 : **Composition of programmes telecast from Hyderabad**

Broad category	Per cent
Sports	24
Feature films & film-based items	23
News & current affairs	18
Developmental programmes (agriculture, health etc.)	10
Music items	8
Plays/Features	8
Others	9

The programmes relayed from Delhi accounted for as much as 70 per cent of the transmission time. It is difficult to escape from Urban-fixation in Delhi programmes. They faithfully reflect Delhi priorities and Delhi personalities. Secondly, they necessarily imply large-scale programme feeding in Hindi and English languages. An analysis of the Hyderabad TV content by languages indicated the following pattern :

Language	*Per cent*
Hindi/Urdu	33
English	32
Telugu	28
Others	7

Figure 2 depicts the station airing from two mouths to keep up its promise to serve the rural masses and the urban masters. The rural poor receive its favours by way of hardcore instructional programmes, soft core enrichment plays and entertaining

TWO FACES OF
UPAGRAHA DOORDARSHAN

Fig. 2.

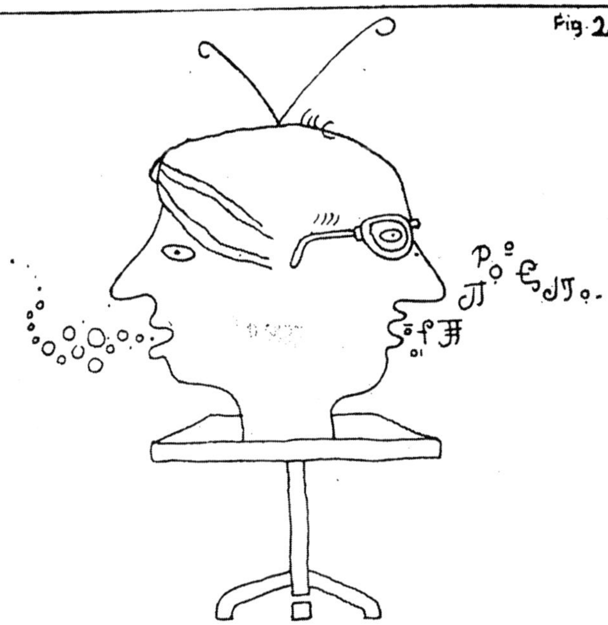

- JAI SANTOSHIMA (Hindi Film)
- HYBRID SOTHI
- TAGUDU DOSHAM (Play) (Effects of alcohol)
- FOLK DANCES
- ALLAM MURABBA (For women)

- BANDODU-GUNDAMMA (Telugu Film)
- KRISHNA LEELA (Ballet)
- Bharatanatyam
- Moolugulu Muchatlu
- VARTALU
- DELHI DURBAR
- SAMACHAR
- HARYANA PEACE MARCH
- CALCUTTA SAMMELAN

films. The urban rich are fed with sumptuous delicacies in exciting colours, from Wimbledon, Lahore, Los Angeles, New York, London, Bombay and Delhi.

PROGRAMMES FOR WOMEN AND CHILDREN

Field report from Jeedimetla

Jeedimetla is a small village with a population of less than [illegible],000 persons, about 20 kms. away from Hyderabad. It lies in the industrial belt, outside the urban agglomeration, in Medchal taluka of Ranga Reddy district. The village has a high school, where the Community TV set (VHF) is located. The custody of the set is entrusted to the Record Assistant in the school, but he in turn delegated the responsibility to a watchman in the same school.

Personal enquiries with school children and others in nearby households revealed that the TV set has not been functioning for the past 4-5 months. Last month, the maintenance department carried out some repairs, but again it went out of order.

As a general rule, when the set is in working condition, the watchman switches it on for the weekly Telugu and Hindi feature films. Thus, on Saturdays and Sundays a large crowd of 250-300 gathers at the high school. Frequently, youngsters bring pressure on the watchman for other film-based items like Chitrahaar and Chitramala. He allows them to operate the set. Otherwise, it rémains closed.

In the case of teleschool (ETV) programmes, it is reported that seldom are the children allowed to watch, though some teachers do assemble at the set to have a glimpse of the programmes.

These observations indicate that children and women hardly have any exposure to the programme telecast for their benefit. However, a small group of children from the village could recollect a few "do-it-yourself" type of programmes which they enjoyed watching on TV at a school adjacent to their village. Here the headmaster is said to take pains to personally monitor the set and arrange group-viewing. He encourages the children by giving gifts for the models prepared by them.

Reports from Rudraram

Rudraram is a village with about 2,500 population in Medak district, 10 kms. away from the BHEL township, Ramachandrapuram. The community TV—the only set in the village—is located in the Gram Panchayat Office, which also houses a Balwadi centre. It was installed five years ago. The watchman of the primary school is the official custodian, but all the members of his family operate the set.

On the day of the visit, the set was not in working order. It was gathered from the villagers that it broke down about six months back. During the first week of November, the maintenance department repaired the set and the villagers availed of the opportunity to watch the programmes telecast soon after Mrs. Gandhi's assassination. However, the set broke down once again within a week's time.

Normally, when the set is in good condition, it is kept open throughout the transmission time from 7.00 p.m. to 10.30 p.m. However, not more than 5-10 adults and 15-20 children assemble at the set. It was pointed out that females (above the age of 13 years and particularly those who attended schools/ colleges) never come to watch the programmes. The main reason for their avoidance is said to be the presence of eve-teasers and mischief-makers among the viewers. However, the feature films telecast on Saturdays and Sundays are reported to attract large audiences of 300-400 people.

Only two women in a group of fifteen could recollect a progrnmme on "Healthy food" telecast recently in the womens' programme. The recollection of items among the children was, however, very poor.

Report from Warangal*

Warangal receives Delhi programmes directly from the satellite through the LPT. The audience, therefore, gets a variety of programmes both in Hindi and English languages specifically designed for children. They include story-telling sessions, short films, quiz programmes, plays, magic shows, puppet shows, etc. The duration of the programmes varies

*Report received on request from Kum. Sadhana Vemuganti.

between 15-30 minutes. The Sunday morning shows provide a package of entertainment for the children.

The reception of the programmes relayed through satellite is very unsatisfactory at Warangal. The picture becomes hazy and many set owners are quite unhappy with the transmission.

The viewers' assessment of the programmes is that they are meaningful with a fair amount of education and entertainment. Programmes for and by children are particularly considered to be attractive. In this connection, mention was made for a programme in which a little boy interviewed two little children—a classical singer and a ballerina dancer. Though Hindi films like *Meera* were liked for their educative value, the children evinced more interest in the cartoon films.

The story telling sessions for children, however, did not find audience favour. The participating children in the programme were considered to be too young to understand the stories. One important observation was that the plays for and by children were comparatively few and far between.

Programmes for women are presented, once a week under the title *Mahilaon ke liye*. The package includes items on cookery, handicrafts, talks, health and family welfare, beauty care, etc. There is nothing special about them and they are in the usual package dished out for women on the radio pattern.

RURAL INDIA IS NOT IN THE PICTURE

J.S. Srivastava

THE TV network in the country is spreading rapidly due to the quick implementation of Doordarshan's special expansion plan. Consequently, the reach of TV is going to increase from 20 per cent to 70 per cent of the population by the end of this year, through several high power and low power transmitters. Programmes in Hindi and English from Doordarshan Kendra, Delhi, are being shown in the areas covered by these transmitters throughout the country, mainly to rural audiences. However, such programmes, which include imported film and video material, are geared to the needs and tastes of urban audiences and not to those of the rural masses.

Thus, they defeat the main objective of TV as defined by the government which is "to assist in the process of social and economic development and to act as an effective medium for providing information, education and entertainment", specifically in rural areas.

Why has this situation arisen ? We all know that TV was started by the government with the main objective of accelerating the process of development. Despite so many changes in the plans and priorities of the government with regard to the development and expansion of TV during the 25 years of its existence, there has been no shift in the policy of the government as far as the developmental purpose of TV is concerned. However, if one objectively reviews the performance of TV during this period, it becomes quite evident that there has been a shift from the original intention of using it as a medium for education and development, since it has been dominated by poor quality entertainment programmes aimed at pleasing urban viewers.

A widening gap

Let us examine the reason for this widening gap between policy and performance in the context of the INSAT project, conceived and implemented in order to accelerate the process of development, particularly in remote rural areas of the country.

The utilisation plan of the TV segment of INSAT envisages the beaming of development-oriented TV programmes in the target areas on the pattern of SITE, which was the largest experiment in developmental communication to have been conducted in the world. These programmes have to be made according to the specific needs of the target audience, with the participation of the local people and in their language or dialect, if they are to be effective. To meet the needs of this kind of local programming, it was found imperative to decentralise production facilities. Accordingly, plans have already been made to set up base production studios in places like Hyderabad, Cuttack, Gorakhpur, Nagpur, Rajkot and Ranchi.

If we take stock of the actual utilisation of the TV segment of INSAT, it is evident that it is the programming area that is most lacking. This is clear from the fact that during the period when INSAT-1A was fully operational, it could not be utilised for telecasting original programmes in the nine districts of Andhra Pradesh, Orissa and Maharashtra covered by the first phase of the utilisation plan of INSAT. The reason for this was that the programmes were simply not ready.

Unfortunately, INSAT-1A failed in the sky. This provided adequate time for planning and preparing programmes for INSAT-1B, which was launched after a gap of about one year, in August 1983. However, this, too, was not done. The studios planned for Gorakhpur, Ranchi, Rajkot and Nagpur as part of the second and third phase utilisation plan of INSAT were not fully operational. Consequently, the Area specific programmes which were to originate from the studios were not ready, though INSAT-1B was a year old on August 30, 1984. Thus, it is evident that programmes from Doordarshan Kendra, Delhi, were being telecast through these new transmitters in remote rural areas, not perhaps, as a matter of policy but out of compulsion, since local-based programmes were not ready, and therefore, not available for transmission.

Lack of software planning

This style of functioning adopted by Doordarshan, where efforts are concentrated on meeting immediate crises and where long-term goals are overshadowed, is primarily due to a lack of software planning and management at both the directorate and TV station levels. Software planning and the management of a fast-moving creative medium like television which involves multiple resources and complex operations, demands speedy action and relative freedom from the structural and procedural ills of bureaucracy. There is, therefore, a paramount need to depart from traditional ways of functioning and to introduce and adopt new and dynamic concepts and techniques of management in this field.

This is particularly important at this juncture because Doordarshan is facing the most challenging period in its 25 years of existence with major projects like INSAT, the national programme, colour TV, the second channel, the special expansion plans, etc. being implemented almost simultaneously.

Working group

In order to tackle this problem, the Ministry of Information and Broadcasting recently appointed a working group with Dr. P.C. Joshi as Chairman to prepare a software plan for Doordarshan. The working group has already submitted its report. Unfortunately, the government has not yet released the report and the details of the recommendations made by the group are not known to the public.

However, from reports appearing in newspapers, it is evident that the working group has found that no improvement in software is possible in the existing framework—the present management and style of Doordarshan hampers creativity and initiative at all levels. The group has therefore recommended the restructuring of Doordarshan along the lines of the Atomic Energy and Space Commission. This is a significant recommendation, but making structural changes at the level of the Ministry of Information and Broadcasting and the Doordarshan directorate is a complex task, and might take considerable time to implement.

What I personally feel would be feasible even within the existing set-up, is to change the structure and working of the TV stations, making them more responsive to the peculiar needs and problems of TV programme production.

Structural changes

This can be done with the introduction of simple management concepts like planning, organising, leading and controlling as the basis of functioning of TV stations at all levels. The TV stations are the nerve centres of Doordarshan ; they transform policies into realities. The management of TV stations along efficient lines, to facilitate the production of the right type of programmes at minimum cost, is therefore of primary importance.

One of the valuable findings of SITE, now accepted in all quarters, is that any programme produced with developmental objectives for a target audience has to be research-based in order to be relevant and meaningful. The production of such programmes demands a management system which can facilitate research and innovation by providing scope for multidisciplinary teams consisting of producers, researchers, scriptwriters, subject experts ; differing production requirements for various types of programmes ; sufficient lead time for each programme ; creative freedom to producers ; team spirit and technological developments.

At the same time, the system has to be such as to ensure regular and sufficient outputs to meet transmission commmitments.

Experience shows that the existing bureaucratic structure and management system of Doordarshan stations is not capable of meeting these requirements ; they are generally organised and managed along the lines of radio stations. Radio, being a separate medium, finds inbuilt strengths in its particular system of functioning. However, such a system is not suitable even for routine television productions because television is basically a visual medium which involves techniques, equipment, personnel, facilities and aesthetic qualities for programme production that are different from radio.

A management system for TV

Where a management system for TV is concerned, there is no special model which can be followed and adopted. It is not possible here to go into the details of alternative systems. However, it would be useful to recall the attempt that was made to create an organisational structure and management system to suit the complex operations and peculiar problems of production and rural development-oriented programmes for the Pij station (Space Applications Centre, ISRO, Ahmedabad) during SITE.

The system succeeded in meeting production targets for the transmission of locally produced developmental programmes in Gujarati. The system was also able to facilitate high quality work and team work, while permitting a great deal of creative freedom to producers. Thus, the efficacy of this system as an R&D-cum-production-cum transmission mode of operation of a local TV station for rural development has been proved.

It is therefore suggested that the experiences gained in the organisation and management of the Pij station could be beneficially utilised to shape the structure and working of the new TV production centres coming up during INSAT, since both have similar aims and modes of operation. This would enable these INSAT stations to produce and present relevant, high quality programmes for target audiences, and would take TV closer to achieving its prime objective—rural development.

RECOMMENDATIONS

1. THERE is need for an overall Credo that lays down the broad philosophy and policy that will guide all programme production. It should be specific enough to serve as a touch-stone to decide whether a programme proposal or script fits into the framework of the Credo or not.

2. Equally, there is need for an overall philosophy or Credo for the total *transmission,* so as to ensure that sponsored or ready-made programmes (e.g. films) do not directly or indirectly propagate attitudes and values contrary to those laid down in the Credo.

3. These Credos should not merely exist on paper : a sustained effort should be made to sensitise both policy-makers and programme production personnel to their letter and spirit. They should be widely publicised, so that the viewing public too is aware of them.

4. In order that the Credo is implemented, it is essential that appropriate formal mechanisms be set up to promote and monitor adherence to it at programme planning, scripting and pre-transmission stages.

5. There is urgent need to sensitise policy-makers and programme makers (including not only Producers, but also writers and researchers) on issues related to women and children.

6. It is desirable to have separate, dedicated production teams for children's programmes, so as to ensure continuity and accumulation of experiences.

7. Most programmes must be audience, area and language specific to be really effective. This entails local programme production and local transmission, with clearly defined "target" groups (in terms of sex, age, socio-economic, cultural and educational background, etc.). Programmes on the national network too could be useful ; however, in this case the problems related to linguistic comprehension and cultural

identification need to be borne in mind.

8. It will be desirable and beneficial to involve outside agencies ("specialist" agencies—whether official or non-governmental—voluntary agencies, etc.) in programme conception, content/research inputs and programme utilization.

9. Appropriate "user" agencies and voluntary groups should also be encouraged to take up programme production. For this purpose, arrangements should be made for training their personnel, especially to be able to plan and conceptualise programmes and to provide the required content and research inputs. For actual production, however, it is desirable that they use professional cameramen, editors, etc.

10. The experience of voluntary groups and field agencies should be fully used as research and content inputs for defining programme plans, contents and approaches. Not only will this reduce the load on existing researchers, but will bring in fresh and down-to earth inputs.

11. In recruiting personnel, production agencies should assess not only knowledge and skill levels (which, in any case, can be imparted through training and gained by experience), but special emphasis should be placed on the candidates' value-orientation in relation to the Credo.

12. The curricullum of training courses for production personnel should be modified to include sensitivity to and understanding of issues related to women and children. While initially this may be an "add-on" to the present curricullum, the effort should be to make it an integral part rather than an appendage.

13. "User" agencies - especially governmental ones—should have a small cell that acts as a link between the broadcasting agency and the field workers. This cell should itself take on some utilisation activities.

14. For effective programme utilisation, a "campaign approach" should be followed on an intensive, selective and periodical basis. The utilisation cells (mentioned above) should play a vital role in this.

15. Greater "non-broadcast" use of video should be made, especially by "user" agencies, in view of some obvious advantages. Audio cassettes could also be used as a support to video material. Some of the programmes developed for

non-broadcast use should be transmitted and research undertaken to understand the relative advantages and assess the impact of the two different modes (transmission and non-broadcast).

16. Despite its obvious difficulties, there is no alternative to community viewing as a means of ensuring access to the medium for all. Therefore, there is urgent need to rapidly and dramatically increase the number of community sets, including those in schools. The equally urgent problem of maintenance and operation of these sets must also be tackled on an immediate basis. Arrangements for replacing old sets are also essential.

17. Since teacher intervention is necessary for the school broadcasts, steps should be taken to ensure that proper training and orientation is provided to the teachers.

18. Training of teachers in new methods and approaches to teaching can be done on a large-scale using TV in conjunction with other media, as was done during SITE. Full use must be made of this potential, not only for teachers but also for other functionaries concerned with children and women (e.g. Anganwadi workers, ANM's etc.). Both transmission and non-transmission modes could be used for such training.

19. Keeping in mind the sensitivity of certain issues and the likely composition of the audience in relation to the time of the day, a strategy for scheduling of such programmes must be worked out.

20. Efforts should be made to develop a complete annotated bibliography of all research and studies in this field. Similarly, an "annotated bibliography" of all video/film material would be extremely useful. Standard formats for the collection of this information should be prepared and distributed to all production and research agencies. A means of ensuring access to this information is necessary, and it is desirable that some agency take up the job of acting as a focal and co-ordinating agency.

21. A list of issues (and their relative priorities for programme making should be prepared and circulated to all production organisations.

22. In view of the shortage of trained research personnel, priorities for research should be laid down. For the same

reason, it may not be practically feasible—even though it is undoubtedly desirable—to have detailed, formal research inputs for all programmes. However, this constraint can be overcome by resorting to alternatives like getting inputs from field agencies, brain-storming with research and content experts, etc.

23. A complete review of all research studies in these fields is essential. Further, an effort should be made to convert research findings into operational guidelines for Producers. put down in language comprehensive to the Producer.

24. In order to ensure and promote creativity the necessary organisational climate is essential. Work is required to define the structures and mechanisms that will promote "organisational creativity", facilitate teamwork, foster and promote the "right" values.

PLAN OF ACTION

[EACH ACTION item should have one or more persons/agencies responsible for its implementation and a target date for completion. In the case of multiple responsibilities, the first named individual/agency will have primary responsibility.]

1. The Credos for production and transmission should be drafted, circulated to a few interested individuals and finalised. They should then be sent to all production agencies and to Doordarshan for comments and later adoption [??, Jan. 15,1985].

2. A Workshop of a few selected individuals should be organised to prepare a "curricullum" and identify material for sensitisation of production pesonnel to issues relating to women and children. The workshop should also prepare a video-tape for sensitising policy-makers who will not have time to attend a Workshop. [?? March 1985].

3. A list of competent voluntary agencies and individuals working in these fields should be prepared, and sent to production agencies so that they can involve them in production [?? January 1985].

4. Training of personnel from voluntary agencies to be arranged [UNICEF ; on-going].

5. A yearly Workshop and viedo festival, bringing together people and programmes in those areas (it may be better to separate the women's and children's programmes) should be organised. The first such Workshop should be in-1985 at-[??].

6. Documentation of experiences should be encouraged by all agencies concerned. A focal agency should take responsibility for promoting, collating and distributing documentation [??].

7. Appropriate steps should be taken to modify the training curricullum to include the development of understanding and sensitivity with regard to issues about women and children [DECU, FTII, DD ; March 1985].

8. Appropriate funding should be provided to voluntary and non-official agencies to use video in the non-broadcast mode. Separate funds should also be made available to research the impact of broadcast and non-broadcast programmes [??].

9. A detailed analysis of community viewing should be undertaken and recommendations made to ensure its success with regard to set operation and maintenance [??].

10. The preparation of annotated bibliographies for research studies and programmes must be ensured and a central focal/co-ordinating agency identified for collation and dissemination [??].

11. A major effort to analyse research findings and to translate them into operational guidelines for Producers is to be promoted [??].

12. A study on organisational structures and management procedures/mechanisms suitable to India, for production of women's and children's programmes is to be carried out, and suitable alternatives recommended [??].

SEMINAR ON "SITE" TO "INSAT" : PRODUCTION OF PROGRAMMES FOR WOMEN AND CHILDREN, HELD AT SPACE APPLICATIONS CENTRE, AHMEDABAD, NOVEMBER 26–28, 1984

List of Participants

1. Dr Mira B Aghi
   P-14, Green Park Extn.
   New Delhi 110016
2. Dr K K Verma
   A.N. Sinha Institute of
   Social Studies
   Patna 8000001
3. Professor P Bhaskaran
   Indian Institute of
   Management
   Bannerghatta Road
   Bangalore 560075
4. Professor K E Eapen
   14 Dacosta Layout
   Cooke Town
   Bangalore 500084
5. Mr G D Shukul
   Consultant
   Central Institute of
   Educational Technology
   NCERT
   Sri Aurobindo Marg
   New Delhi 110016
6. Dr Kuldip Kumar
   Deptt. of Educational
   Psychology, NCERT
   Sri Aurobindo Marg
   New Delhi 110016
7. Mr G J Pinto
   UNICEF
   Ravindra Masion
   F Vacha Road
   Bombay 400020
8. Mr T P Balagopalan
   Project Officer
   UNICEF
   29, Josier Street
   Nungambakkam
   Madras 600034
9. Professor Yash Pal
   Secretary
   Science & Technology
   Technology Bhavan
   New Mehrauli Road
   New Delhi 110016
10. Prof J S Srivastava
    Film & Television Inst. of
    India
    Law College Road
    Pune 410001
11. Ms Leela Rado
    Deptt. of Communication
    Bangalore University
    125 UVCE, K R Circle
    Bangalore 560001
12. Dr Anita Dighe
    Council for Social
    Development
    53 Lodi Estate
    New Delhi 110003

13. Dr B S S Rao
Faculty Member
(Commn.)
SITE Institute
Yousufguda
Hyderabad 500045
14. Mr Gopal Gupta
5/574 Lodi Colony
New Delhi 110003
15. Dr J K Doshi
Professor & Head
Department of Agril.
Commn.
Pantnagar University
Nainital, UP 263145
16. Ms Neeraja Vohra
Producer
Upagrah Doordarshan
Kendra
Doordarshan
New Delhi 110001
17. Mr Daniel J O'Dell
UNICEF
73 Lodi Estate
New Delhi 110003
18. Ms Chandita Mukherjee
6, Somerset House
Opp. Coloba Post Office
Bombay 400005
19. Ms Rina Gill
UNICEF
T-18 Green Park
New Delhi 110016
20. Ms Anju Daswani
Gazdar House
2nd floor
Bombay 40000
21. Mr Krishan Sondhi
Adviser
Planning Commission
Yojana Bhawan
New Delhi 110001
22. Ms Anupama Rao
UNICEF
73 Lodi Estate
New Delhi 110003
23. Mr A Sai Prasad
All India Radio
Navrangpura
Ahmedabad
24. Ms Dinaz Kalwachwala
Producer
Space Applications Centre
Ahmedabad 380053
25. Professor Vimal Shah
Deptt. of Sociology
Gujarat University
Navrangpura
Ahmedabad 380009
26. Dr R B Lal
Tribal Research Instt.
Gujarat Vidyapath
Ahmedabad 380014
27. Ms Neela Trivedi
16, Gandhi Kunj Soc
Ellisbridge
Ahmedabad 380006
28. Ms Barbara Kolucki
UNICEF
73 Lodi Estate
New Delhi 110003
29. Mr Jahnu Baruah
16, Ganga Vihar
'C' Road Church Gate
Bombay 400020
30. Ms Sindhu Phadke
UNICEF
Calcutta

31. Mr Peter Chen
UNICEF
73, Lodi Estate
New Delhi 110003
32. Mr Dhiran Avashia
Educational Media
Research Centre
Gujarat University
Navrangpura
Ahmedabad 380009
33. Professor E V Chitnis
Director
Space Applications Centre
Ahmedabad 380053
34. Dr Binod C Agrawal
DECU/ISRO
Space Applications
Centre
Ahmedabad 380053
35. Mr K S Karnik
Director
DECU/ISRO
Space Applications Centre
Ahmedabad 380053
36. Dr Arbind K Sinha
DECU/ISRO
Space Applications Centre
Ahmedabad 380053
37. Mr K Vishwanath
Producer
DECU/ISRO
Space Applications Centre
Ahmedabad 380053
38. Mr G C Jain
Space Applications Centre
Ahmedabad 380053
39. Mr S P Jain
DECU/ISRO
Space Applications Centre
Ahmedabad 380053
40. Mr D R Wakharikar
DECU/ISRO
Space Applications Centre
Ahmedabad 380053
41. Mr Subhash Sehgal
DECU/ISRO
Space Applications Centre
Ahmedabad 380053
42. Mr B S Bhatia
DECU/ISRO
Space Applications Centre
Ahmedabad 380053
43. Mr H J Baradi
DECU/ISRO
Space Applications Centre
Ahmedabad 380053
44. Mr S R Joshi
DECU/ISRO
Space Applications Centre
Ahmedabad 380053
45. Mr A R Dasgupta
Space Applications Centre
Ahmedabad 380053
46. Mr V N Raina
DEDU/ISRO
Space Applications Centre
Ahmedabad 380053

OBSERVERS

1. Ms Hansha Joshi
   DECU/ISRO
   Space Applications Centre
   Ahmedabad 380053
2. Mr K M Parmar
   DECU/ISRO
   Space Applications Centre
   Ahmedabad 380053
3. Ms Bela Trivedi
   DECU/ISRO
   Space Applications Centre
   Ahmedabad 380053
4. Mrs Manjari Shah
   DECU/ISRO
   Space Applications Centre
   Ahmedabad 380053
5. Ms Radha Misra
   DECU/ISRO
   Space Applications Centre
   Ahmedabad 380053
6. Mr S A Vora
   Centre for Development
   Communication
   Gujarat University
   Ahmedabad 380009
7. Ms Karuna Krishna
   National Institute of
   Design
   Paldi
   Ahmedabad 380006

"SITE" TO "INSAT" : PRODUCTION OF PROGRAMMES FOR WOMEN AND CHILDREN

November 26-28, 1984

Group Distribution

Group—A	Group—B	Group—C
K L Sondhi	K E Eapen	Vimal Shah
B S S Rao	Leela Rao	K Vishwanath
J S Srivastava	Anupama Rao	V N Raina
K K Verma	S R Joshi	S Sehgal
P Bhaskaran	Neeraja Vohra	Arbind Sinha
Anita Dighe	Anju Daswani	R B Lal
Gopal Gupta	G J Pinto	Sai Prasad A
Chandita Mukherjee	Dinaz Kalwachwala	K M Parmar
Jahnu Barua	B S Bhatia	Hansha Joshi
Rina Gill	D R Wakharikar	E V Chitnis
Barbara Kolucki	Bela Trivedi	Kuldip Kumar
Karuna Krishna	S A Vora	Mira Aghi
Manjari Shah	Daniel J O'Dell	Radha Misra
K S Karnik	J K Doshi	S P Jain
	T P Balagopalan	G C Jain
	H J Baradi	S Phadke
		Peter Chen

INDEX

Abortion cases, details of, 35
Adequate Communication, 33
Aghi, Mira B., 19, 86
Agrawal, Binod C., 3, 25, 44, 69, 86
Agricultural programmes, 28
Ahilya (Serial), 91
Ahmedabad, 162; Space Application Centre, 6, 67
All-India Educational Survey, 118
All-India Radio, 47, 128
Alternative educational system, 98
American Commercial TV, 83
Anantapur, 139
Andhra Pradesh, 83, 109
Anganwadi workers, 127, 129, 158
Animal husbandry programme, 25, 69, 137
Asiane Passenger Payload Experiment (APPLE), 14
Atomic Energy and Space Commission, 153
Audience Research Units, 27; profile of, 26
Audio-visual media, 33; nature, 49
Axiliary Nurse Midwifes, 127

Bachchan, Amitabh, 7
Balagopalan, T.P., 127
Balasevikas, 127, 129
Balwadi Centre, 149
Bangalore, 131
Beechaganahalli villages, 37
Bhabha, Dr. 12
Bhatia, B.S., 3, 132
Bhaskaran, P., 32, 68
Bihar, 83, 109
Blood banking, 7
Bombay Doordarshan, 20, 21; SITE Studio, 81
Breast feeding practices, 35

Centre for Women's Development Studies (CWDS), 90
Chadiya (Serial), 84, 85
Chattisgarh, 83
Child delivery, place of, 38; development, 25, 58; mortality, 35
Children's film society, 70; programmes, 4, 87, 88, 116, 133, 135; supplementary diet for, 36; Television Workshop (CTW), 3
Chitnis, E.V., 1, 2, 3, 5, 12, 13, 14
Chingleput, 131
Chowdhary, S.V.S., 121
Chullahs, smokeless, 8
Commercial world, 46
Communication environment, 54; export, 64; media, 89; research decade of, 25, 27, 29; systems, 54; Technology, 56; Training, 84
Conference on Research and Evaluation for Executive Decision-making for Education Media (CREDEM), 9
Cuddapah, 139
Cultural heritage, 92
Cunning alliance, 9
Cuttack, 88, 152

Dahisar, 22
Daswane, Anju, 81
Delhi, 14, 42, 45, 88, 113, 114; Doordarshan Kendra, 151; programmes, 146
Development and education, original objectives of, 43; guidance, 58; objectives, 23; programmes, 122
Diarrhoea, 37
Dibhur, 39
Dixit, Varsha, 94, 95
Dogmatic approach, 46

Doordarshan corridors, 27, 43, 61, 109, 154, 160
Doshi, J.K., 42
Draupadi, 91

Eapen, K.E., 47
Educational, vocationalization of, 56, 59; programme, 28, 58, 96; system, 88; technology facilities, 60
Entertainment programmes, 70
ETV, 99
Exemplary educational programme, 83
Experiment, social objectives, 29
Export Group meetings, 58

Family planning works, 25, 41; welfare, 103
Field-based programmes, 50
Food habits, 40

Gandhi, Indira, 11
Garba, 91
Garbadiyo Gattu, 85
Gharelu Ilaj (household remedies), 69
Gram Panchayat office, 149
Grama Sevika, 129
Gorakhpur, 152
Gujarat, 67, 83, 116

Health Care delivery system, 33; management, 32; functionaries, 36; and nutrition, 25
Human and animal waste, disposal of, 39; communication, 121
Humlog (Serial), 91
Hyderabad, 138, 141, 142; 144, Upagraha Doordarshan Kendra, 146

ICCTR—UNICEF Delhi, 49
IDIOT Box, 79
Indian National Satellite, (INSAT), 1, 2, 6, 7, 66 71, 98, 120, 166; INSAT-III, 15 54, 71; INSAT-IB, 109, 152; Children's programme, 23; framework, 29; programmes, 33, 67; project, 152; software planners, 38; television, 3; television signals, 123; television system, 2
Indian Remote Sensing Satellite, 14
Indian Space Research Organisation, (ISRO) 1, 5, 12, 14, 46, 141
Infant mortality rate, 132
Information and Broadcasting Ministry, 7; and entertainment programmes, 51
Infrastructural facilities, 95
Instructional materials, preparation of, 59
Integrated approach, 96
INTELSAT, 12
Inter-personal Communication, 123
Ismailpur (Bihar), 67

Jagine Joun to, 134
Jai Amarnath, 91
Jai Santoshi Ma (a Hindi feature film), 92
Jolpari, 85
Jeedimetla, 148
Joshi, P.C., 109, 153

Kalwachwala, Dinaz, 89
Kamasamudram village, 37
Karimnagar, 139
Karnataka, 23, 32, 39, 109, 140
Karmik, K.S., 3, 137
Karvachoth, 91
Kerala, 130
Kerala Shastra Sahitya Parishad, 101
Kheda, 85; audience, 116; communication project, 66, 70, 92; operation cell, 83; programme planning stages of, 8; school-education programmes, 138; Transmission, 42, 45
Kishore Bharati, 101
Kolucki, Barbara, 3
Krishi Darshan, 12, 45
Krishnamurthy, P.V., 14

Kumar, Kuldip, 56
Kurnool, 139

Levin, Lowell, 106
LHVs, 38
Literacy programmes, 100
Lower Power Transmitter (LPT), 13, 144, 149

Madhya Pradesh, 22
Madras Doordarshan, 131
Mahabubnagar, 131
Mahila Mandal, 93, 129, 135
Mahilaon ke liye, 150
Malek, M.R., 86
Malnutrition, maladies of, 105
Mass Communication, 33, 36
Master Pritam, 91
Medak, 149
Media credibility, 53
Meera (Hindi film), 150
Middle class urban women, 90
Monolithic programming, 30
Mukherjee, Chandite, 88

Nagpur, 152
Nandu-Indu, 133
Nari-Tun-Narayani, 93, 94, 97, 134
National Aeronautics Space Administration (NASA), 12
National Council of Educational Research and Training (NCERT) 12; academic assistance, 60; councelling and guidance of, 57
National Network, 88; policy, objectives of, 100; programmes, 131
Natural environment, 101
Negatives programmes, 136
Nehru, Jawaharlal, 12
Nellore, 138
New Delhi, 59
NIKY TASHA, 70
Nitty gritty, 30
Nyay-Anyay, 94, 95

Organisations, non-governmental, 5
Orissa, 22, 78, 83
Orthodox traditional society, 86
Overal credo, 136; programme, 156

Pal, Yash, 2, 5, 6, 7, 8, 9, 11, 14
Parental participation, 56
Parvati, 91
Periodic medical examination, 39
Pij experiment, 88; station, 14, 155; transmitter, 13, 83, 92
Pondicherry, 130
Post-natal problems, 105
Pre-telecast or post-telecast, 44
Pre-transmission feedback, 77
Primary education, universalization of, 57
Programme, syllabus-oriented packages of, 52; utilisation of, 113; variety of, 27
Public broadcasting, 55

Quality programme production, 27
Quick feedback, 21
Quiz programmes, 101

Raina, V.N., 103
Rajahmundry, 139
Rajasthan, 83, 108
Rajkot, 152
Ranchi, 152
Rao, Leela, 62
Rao, B.S.S., 138
Research jargons, 30
Rural American child, 79; audiences, 49, 51, 70, 119; children, 22, 42; communication, 64, 121; development, 25, 46, 50; Indian child, 79; TV programmes, 50, 121

Sambalpur, 78, 83
Sarabhai, Vikram, 12, 109
Satellite based television system, 66; communication, 12; technology, 26
Satellite Instructional Television Experiment (SITE), 4, 24, 25, 32, 42, 46, 48, 66, 119, 121, 139, 141, 158, 166; children's programme, 20, 22; experience 47, 52, 62, 110; experiment, 110; communication,

48; philosophy, 64; science programme, 4
Satellite Telecommunications Experiments Project (STEP), 14
Science education programme, 19, 20, 75, 82, 119; and technology, 46
Sati-Sita, 91
School-learning-environment, 57
Sesane street, 26, 82, 83, 113
Shah, Madhuriben, 14
Sharma, B.V., 139
Shukla, G.D., 108
Sinha, Arbind, 66, 68, 69
Sixth Five Year Plan, 139
Socio-economic class, 30; status, software planning, 122, 153
Social Welfare Gramsevikas, 127
Space Application Centre, 75, 92, 155, 175; Technology, 89
Special target groups, 27
Srivastava, J.S., 151
State Bureaus of Educational and Vocational Guidance, 59, 60
Sunday bazar, 79
Syllabus based courses, problems in, 68

Tamil Nadu, 32, 130
Target audience, 75, 76, 77
Technology-dictated communication, 55
Teleschool (ETV) programmes, 148
Terrestrial transmitters, 121
Thanjavur farmers, 48
Third Five Year Plan, 12
Tirupati, 139
Training programmes, 29; strategy, 59, 61
Transportation and communication facilities, 49
Trivandrum, 131
TV, on policy for future, 49; educational programme, 26, 118; network, 96; operational system, 1; programmes, 32 research utilisation, 53, 54; viewing and radio listening facilities, 60

Unfamiliar communication technology, 62
UNESCO, 1, 3, 5, 114, 160
UNICEF participants, 2
University Grant Commission, (UGC), 49
Upgrah Doordarshan Kendras, 122
Urban American child, 79, 85
Utopia, 107

Value Orientation, 7
Very High Resolution Radio meter (VHRR), 13
VHF community TV sets, position of, 144
Video film, bibliography of, 2; programmes packages, 103, 104, 136
Vijayawada, 139, 141
Vikram Hall, 2, 4
Village level mehila mandals, representatives of, 127
Visakhapatnam, 139, 141
Viswanath, K., 3, 14, 116
Vividh Bharathi, 48
Vohra, Neeraja, 121

Warangal, 139, 149, 150
Women and children, programmes for, 4, 6, 68, 86, 87, 122, 135, 148, 161, 166; experiences, 121; researchers, 80

Xavier Institute of communication, 81

Yogabhyas (Yogic exercises), 92